中国古代窑址标本

北京 山东 陕西 宁夏 辽宁

故宫博物院 / 编　冯小琦 / 主编

故宫出版社

THE SPECIMENS OF ANCIENT CHINESE KILNS IN THE COLLECTION OF THE PALACE MUSEUM

BEIJING,SHANDONG,SHAANXI,NINGXIA AND LIAONING VOLUME

COMPILED BY THE PALACE MUSEUM
THE CHIEF COMPILER: FENG XIAOQI

THE FORBIDDEN CITY PUBLISHING HOUSE

凡例

一、本书分卷以省为单位，窑多者，一省单独成册，窑少者，数省成书。

二、每个窑的标本以时代为序，同时兼顾品种、器形、装饰分类排列。

三、在某些重要窑名下，为清楚地表达瓷片的采集地，又分若干小地名。

四、标本的年代参考各地考古发掘资料，资料不充分或有意见分歧者，以故宫博物院传统观点为准。

五、有些标本因器形不完整，时代特征不突出，兼具宋、金或金、元特征者，取其一，或以宋（金）、金至元的形式标出。

六、窑具的年代、时代特征不突出者，或不标年代，或把范围定宽，如金至元，均放在每个窑的最后。

七、书中所选完整器物与窑址标本对比，以附图形式出现。

八、全国窑址分布图中的窑址为历年资料汇集，窑址所在县市地名绝大部分沿用学界习惯称谓。

九、故宫博物院专家窑址调查报告以省区划分，附于本省瓷窑后，有的涉及两省或多省的，附主要省份论文的最后。

Notes on the Use of the Book

1, The different volumes of this series were classified mainly by the provinces, with more kilns in one province done on single book and less one put it together.

2, The specimens of one kiln sorted by time, also considering the variety, type and decorative method.

3, In order to introduce the locality of specimens gathering precisely, the specific place names were also used for some important kilns.

4, The judgment on time of specimens was on the basis of archaeological materials from place to place, and the specimens in dispute or inadequate data were dated by traditional viewpoint of the Palace Museum.

5, Due to the incomplete type, the time character of some specimens was not glowing. The one that has features of Song and Jin dynasty or Jin and Yuan dynasty at the same time was dated in single period, or marked with "Song dynasty (Jin dynasty)" or the time of "from Jin dynasty to Yuan dynasty".

6, The kiln furniture in inconspicuous character of time could not indicate the specific date or broaden the period scale, then put it at last place of the kiln.

7, In contrast, the intact wares in the book appeared in attached figures.

8, Based on the materials over the years, we presented the distribution map of kilns in China, and most of the kiln names were followed by Scholar's idiom.

9, The investigation reports of experts of the Palace Museum were divided by different provinces and attached to the kilns of single province. The reports including two provinces or more attached behind the major province.

序

为加强故宫学术研究，在纪念故宫博物院成立 80 周年之际，建立故宫博物院古陶瓷研究中心，这是很有意义的一件事。

故宫博物院自成立以来，在中国古陶瓷研究方面，具有三个明显的优势：

其一是人才。故宫博物院是在明清皇宫的基础上建立的中国最大的古代艺术品宝库，凭借其得天独厚的条件，曾造就出一大批享誉海内外的文物研究专家。在古陶瓷研究领域，陈万里、孙瀛洲、冯先铭、耿宝昌先生等闻名遐迩，使故宫博物院在这一领域长期独领风骚。今天，在古陶瓷研究专业的人员构成方面，现有本研究专业在职人员 16 人，其中取得研究馆员任职资格的 5 人，副研究馆员任职资格的 4 人，馆员任职资格的 7 人，另有返聘研究馆员 2 人，退休研究馆员 3 人，副研究馆员 1 人，馆员 2 人。特别是拥有当今古陶瓷研究领域的泰斗、现已近 90 岁高龄的耿宝昌先生。因此，无论是在从业人员的数量还是人员的梯队结构方面，故宫博物院在这一研究领域都具有明显的优势。

其二是陶瓷类文物藏品。故宫博物院现收藏的古陶瓷可分为三大类：

1. 陶瓷类文物。总计约 35 万件，其中 32 万多件属原清宫旧藏品，1949 年以后通过拨交、收购、捐献等渠道又入藏 2 万多件。这些藏品，不但数量大，而且精品多，从新石器时代的陶器到明清各朝官民窑瓷器，无不包括，自成体系，这是国内外其他任何博物馆所无法比拟的。其中被初步定为国家一级文物的陶瓷器就有 1 110 件。宋代五大名窑（汝、官、哥、定、钧）瓷器、明清官窑瓷器是故宫陶瓷收藏中的强项，仅以宋代汝窑瓷器，明代永乐、宣德官窑瓷器，清代康熙瓷器为例：国内外收藏传世汝窑瓷器不足百件，故宫收藏 20 件，又收藏明代永乐、宣德官窑瓷器 700 多件，康熙瓷器 7 万多件。这些藏品无论从数量还是质量上看，在世界上都是名列前茅的。

2. 古窑址陶瓷标本。故宫博物院收藏有 20 世纪 50 ～ 60 年代以来从全国各地考察古窑址所采集的 300 余处重要窑址的约 6 万陶瓷标本，这在世界上也是独一无二的。标本的时代上起商周，下至清代，其中以唐到元代窑址的标本最为丰富。有的标本可与出土和传世器物相印证，有的标本则不见于出土与传世器物中。因此，对古窑址陶瓷标本的研究愈发显得重要，它能使我们更清楚地了解我国古代各地烧造陶瓷的情况，补充文献与传世器物的不足。目前有些窑址已遭破坏或深埋于地下，再前往采集标本，已几乎不可能有所收获，因此故宫所藏这批古窑址陶瓷标本就愈显重要。

3. 陶瓷类实物资料。故宫博物院现收藏有原清宫因残淘汰下来的、古物南迁损伤的以及 1949 年以后收购来的数千件基本完整而被划归为非文物的资料，以及清宫淘汰下来的大量明清官窑瓷片标本。这些实物资料数量之大、包含的花色品种之全，在世界上是首屈一指的。其中有大量明、清、民国时期的陶瓷仿品，至今尚未全面向社会公开过，它们是学习古陶瓷鉴定的珍贵资料。特别是资料中还有一些品种弥补了现存古陶瓷文物中的空白。

其三是古陶瓷研究成果。在深入研究的基础上，故宫博物院已先后编写出版的陶瓷类图书有《故宫博物院藏瓷选集》（文物出版社，1962 年）、《故宫珍藏康雍乾瓷器图录》（两木出版社、紫禁城出版社，1989 年）、《故宫博物院藏清盛世瓷选粹》（紫禁城出版社，1994 年）、《故宫藏传世瓷器真赝对比及重要窑址标本图录》（紫禁城出版社，1998 年）、《故宫博物院藏明初青花瓷器》（紫禁城出版社，2002 年）、《故宫博物院藏文物珍品全集》[其中陶瓷类文物九卷：晋唐名瓷一卷、两宋瓷器二卷、五彩斗彩一卷、珐琅彩粉彩一卷、颜色釉一卷、青花釉里红三卷，商务印书馆（香港）有限公司]、《孙瀛洲的陶瓷世界》（紫禁城出版社，2003 年）、《陈万里陶瓷考古文集》（紫禁城出版社、两木出版社，1990 年）、《冯先铭古陶瓷论文集》（紫禁城出版社、两木出版社，1987 年）等。个人专著有陈万里《中国青瓷史略》和《瓷器与浙江》、耿宝昌《明清瓷器鉴定》、李辉柄《中国瓷器鉴定基础》和《宋代官窑瓷器》、叶佩兰《元代瓷器》、王莉英《陶瓷器鉴赏与收藏》、吕成龙《中国古代颜色釉瓷器》和《中国古陶瓷款识》、王健华《古瓷辨赏》等。另外，故宫的陶瓷专业人员还撰写了大量科研论文。这些已出版或发表的故宫专家和学者的研究成果，受到国内外古陶瓷爱好者的广泛关注。特别是 1982 年由冯先铭先生主编的《中国陶瓷史》，堪称我国第一部权威的陶瓷史，赢得国内外陶瓷界的极高赞誉，曾全文译成日文在日本出版。

正因为具备上述丰厚的藏品基础和研究优势，在加强故宫学的学术规划中，成立故宫博物院古陶瓷研究中心被提上了议事日程，在社会同行的支持下，并予以实施。故宫博物院古陶瓷研究中心设在延禧宫区，主要由三部分构成：一是设在延禧宫西司库的观摩室兼作小型会议室；二是设在延禧宫西库房的陶瓷专题陈列室，室内设触摸屏和等离子显示屏；三是设在延禧宫的古陶瓷检测研究中心，内设古陶瓷成份分析实验室，工艺研究实验室，结构分析实验室和物理、化学性质检测实验室，承担古陶瓷的分析检测研究工作。观摩室和小型会议室供来陶瓷中心访问的专家、学者观摩古陶瓷资料、标本以及进行小规模的学术研讨活动等使用。古陶瓷专题陈列室将定期举办院藏陶瓷专题展览，展示故宫古陶瓷专家、学者的研究成果，适当引进一些外展。

故宫博物院古陶瓷研究中心是一个高层次的国际性学术研究机构。该中心将在故宫博物院的领导下，在院学术委员会的指导下，由院古器物部和文保科技部具体负责其日常业务工作，积极开展国内外有关古陶瓷方面的学术研究和学术交流活动。

古陶瓷研究中心的研究对象主要是故宫博物院的古陶瓷收藏、古窑址陶瓷标本收藏和世界各地收藏的中国古代陶瓷。古陶瓷研究中心的研究内容包括对不同时期、不同产地、不同类型古陶瓷制作原料、工艺、结构及相关性质的科学研究；对古陶瓷年代、窑口、真伪的科学研究；对古陶瓷的科学保管、修复和复制等技术的科学研究，以及更多深层次、多视角的科学研究。

古陶瓷研究中心将利用故宫博物院在人才和收藏古陶瓷文物、资料、标本以及引进各种先进检测仪器设备等方面的条件和优势，为国内外专家、学者搭建一个开展综合性合作研究的学术平台，旨在使故宫博物院陶瓷藏品的诸多内涵为世人所知，以弘扬博大精深的中国陶瓷文化。同时，积极借鉴国内外同行的研究方法和学术成果，为故宫培养和造就一批古陶瓷专业的中青年专家，力求使故宫的古陶瓷科学研究水平位于世界的最前列。

为配合古陶瓷研究中心的成立，故宫博物院组织院内专家、学者在深入研究的基础上，将陆续编辑出版《故宫博物院藏清代御窑瓷器》、《故宫博物院藏历代古窑址标本图录》、《故宫博物院藏古陶瓷资料选萃》等三套图书。清代御窑瓷器是故宫收藏中的强项，《故宫博物院藏清代御窑瓷器》一书将收录故宫收藏从顺治至宣统御窑瓷器 1 000 余件，配以大量辅助资料，这是故宫首次出版全面反映清代御窑厂生产工艺及产品的图录，其中绝大多数瓷器属首次公开发表。《故宫博物院藏历代古窑址标本图录》一书，收录故宫自 1949 年以来赴全国各地考察古窑址所采集的 200 多个窑口的陶瓷标本，这是故宫首次向社会全面公布这批标本资料。《故宫博物院藏古陶瓷资料选萃》一书将收录 500 余件故宫藏器形基本完整的古陶瓷实物资料，其中有一部分属于珍稀品种，属于首次发表。我深信，这些古陶瓷图书的出版，必将对中国古陶瓷工艺学、鉴定学的研究起到积极的推动作用。

郑欣淼

2005 年春

Preface

Due to the goal to enhance the academic research level of the Palace Museum, the foundation of Ancient Ceramic Research Center of the Palace Museum was a very significant event during the 80th anniversary of the establishment of the Palace Museum.

The Palace Museum has following three advantages in research on ancient Chinese ceramic since its inception.

Thc first is talents. Based on the imperial palace of Ming and Qing dynasties, the Palace Museum was the largest treasure-house for ancient artworks in China. On account of these exceptional advantages, the Palace Museum brings up a large number of overseas renowned experts on cultural relic research. The well-known experts such as Chen Wanli, Sun Yingzhou, Feng Xianming and Geng Baochang took the Palace Museum lead in the research on ancient ceramic for a long term. Due to enough personned number and reasonable team structure, we still keep the obvious dominant position in the field of ancient ceramic at present.

The second is ceramic collections. The ceramic collections of the Palace Museum could be divided into three classes. One is the cultural relic of ceramic. There were nearly 350 thousands collections, among which over 320 thousands belonged to the Qing Court and the others were collected after 1949 through different approaches. The collections were not only large in number, but also high in quality, and have established a self-contained system from Neolithic Age to Qing dynasty. Then is the specimen of ancient kilns. The Palace Museum collected nearly 60 thousands specimens from over 300 ancient kilns throughout the country in 1950s and 1960s. It was really an unmatched accomplishment in the world. The last is the material of ceramic. The materials contained the following parts: incomplete wares of Qing Court, damaged wares due to removal for antiques, purchased wares as materials after 1949 and large number specimens eliminated by the Qing Court. It is also the second to none in the world.

The third is the research achievement of ancient ceramic. Based on deeply study, the Palace Museum compiled a great deal of ceramic books, such as *The Selected Works of Ceramic in the Collection of Palace Museum* (The Cultural Relic Press, 1962), *The Blue and White Porcelain of Early Ming Dynasty in the Collection of Palace Museum* (The Forbidden City Publishing House, 2002), *The Complete Works of Treasures in the Collection of Palace Museum* (The Hong Kong Commercial Press Ltd., 1996-2000) , *The Ceramic World of Sun Yingzhou* (The Forbidden City Publishing House, 2003), etc. There were also numbers of personal monograph as wall, for example, *The History of Chinese Celadon* (By Chen Wanli, The People's Publishing House, 1965), *The Porcelain and Zhejing Province* (By Chen Wanli, The Zhonghua Book Company, 1964), *The Porcelain*

Appreciation of Ming and Qing Dynasties (The Forbidden City Publishing House, 1993), *The Inscriptions of Ancient Chinese Ceramic* (By Lü Chenglong, The Forbidden City Publishing House, 2003), etc. Besides, large numbers of papers were written by our experts on ceramic and attracted widespread attention.

Based on the abundant collections and research advantages, the establishment of the Ancient Ceramic Research Center of the Palace Museum was put on the agenda and carried out at last. The research center is located at Palace of Prolonged Happiness area, and could be further divided into three parts: small meeting room, ceramic showroom and laboratory for ceramic detection.

The Ancient Ceramic Research Center of the Palace Museum is an international academic research institution at high level. Under the leadership of the Palace Museum and the guidance of Academic Board of the Palace Museum, the Department of Ancient Cultural Relic and Technology for Ancient Cultural Relic Protection will be in charge of daily affairs of the center, and carry out academic research and communication on ancient ceramic in domestic and abroad.

The object of the Ancient Ceramic Research Center of the Palace Museum is the ancient ceramic collections and specimens in the Palace Museum and ancient ceramic collections all over the world. By these condition and advantages, the center will provide experts and scholars with a synthetic platform for academic exchange, and propagate the great and profound culture of Chinese ceramic.

To coincide with the launch of the Ancient Ceramic Research Center of the Palace Museum and on account of further study by experts and scholars in the Palace Museum, some related books will be published such as *The Imperial Porcelain of Qing Dynasty in the Collection of the Palace Museum*, *The Ancient Chinese Kilnsite Specimens* in *the Collection of the Palace Museum* and *The Selected Works of Ancient Ceramic Materials in the Collection of the Palace Museum*. It is convinced that the print of these books will contribute greatly to the development on handicraft and appreciation of ancient Chinese ceramic.

Zheng Xinmiao

目录

Contents

前言

冯小琦

中国陶瓷有8000年的历史，在世界工艺美术史上占有重要位置。半个世纪以来，我国文物考古工作者在20多个省、市、自治区的176个以上县市发现数以千计的历代瓷窑遗址，各地清理发掘的古墓葬也出土了数以万计的历代陶瓷器。新资料与文物的大量出土，为系统研究中国陶瓷的发展历史创造了有利条件。

本套书选用的标本源自20世纪50年代以来，故宫博物院的陶瓷研究专家和学者深入考古第一线，历尽艰辛，陆续在全国调查古窑址所得。特别是老一辈陶瓷专家陈万里、冯先铭、耿宝昌、李辉柄、叶喆民、李知宴、王莉英、叶佩兰等先生，他们在这方面做出了巨大贡献，在这里我们表示特别感谢。

陶瓷考古是一项非常艰巨的工作，瓷窑多依山傍水而建，20世纪50～60年代调查条件非常艰苦，没有汽车，专家们就搭乘拖拉机、马车、驴车，或租自行车，实在没有交通工具就徒步前进，去一处窑址往往要走上一天，他们冒严寒，战酷暑，肩背手提，把获得的第一手珍贵资料带回故宫；在这期间他们有的被蛇咬过，被蝎子蜇过，划破手脚更是经常的事，但是他们凭着对事业的执着，始终坚持深入考古第一线，克服了重重困难，收集了非常宝贵的资料，为故宫博物院的陶瓷研究工作作出了重大贡献。

这些窑址标本资料的时代上起商周，下至明清，系统地反映了中国陶瓷的发展概况以及各地瓷窑产品的特点及相互影响。其中有我国青瓷的发源地——浙江地区商周时期的青瓷、黑瓷和六朝青瓷标本；隋唐时期南、北方地区著名瓷窑邢窑、定窑、巩县窑、耀州窑、越窑、长沙窑等窑的标本；宋代著名瓷窑汝窑、官窑、定窑，钧窑、耀州窑、磁州窑、景德镇窑、龙泉窑、越窑的标本以及福建、广东等沿海地区生产的外销瓷器标本。

这批窑址资料涉及全国20个省区的180余个窑口、300余处窑址，约6万多片标本。其中以唐至元代的标本最为丰富。品种有青釉、白釉、白釉绿彩、黑釉、黄釉、三彩、绞胎、酱釉、黑花、绿釉、红绿彩、釉下褐彩、青白釉、青花等；造型凡生活所用盘、高足盘、碟、碗、高足碗、杯、盆、罐、坛、炉、瓶、壶、枕、灯、盒等应有尽有；装饰所见有划花、刻花、剔花、印花、彩绘、点彩、堆塑、浮雕、镂空等。其中有的标本可与出土和传世器物相印证，有的标本则不见于出土与传世器物。因此，对窑址标本的研究就愈显得重要。作为资料它能使我们更清楚地了解每个瓷窑生产的内涵，补充文献与传世器物的不足。尤其是目前有些窑址已遭破坏或深埋于地下，再前往采集标本，已难有收获，因此，这批标本就愈显珍贵。

故宫博物院收集的陶瓷标本，不论数量上还是质量上在全国都是名列前茅的。其中有些标本曾在英国、日本、香港等国家和地区展出，引起很大轰动，在世界范围内对中国陶瓷的研究起到了积极的推动作用。多年以来，全国各地的陶瓷工作者来故宫博物院参观学习，都曾希望故宫博物院能把这批窑址标本公开展示，并且出版，不少陶瓷爱好者和观众也希望能一睹故宫博物院这批收藏。为满足专业研究人员及广大观众的愿望，并为故宫博物院古陶瓷研究中心建立一个展示平台，我们将数十年调查的窑址标本全面地加以展示，期待它对于我国陶瓷的深入研究能够起到一定推动作用。本套书拟从 6 万多片陶瓷器标本中遴选 180 余个窑口、300 余处窑址的约一万余片古窑址标本进行展示，力求反映我国陶瓷的发展历史，同时也反映故宫博物院几十年来在陶瓷考古方面所取得的成就，弘扬我国的陶瓷文化，并藉以推动古陶瓷研究的深入。

Foreword

Feng Xiaoqi

The Chinese ceramic with a history over 8000 years was one of the most important inventions in China and occupied an outstanding position in the history of arts and crafts in the world. Our workers of cultural relic and archaeology excavated thousands of ancient kilns and tombs and discovered millions of ceramic specimens during half a century. The new materials provide us with useful advantage for study of ceramic systematically.

The selected specimens of the books were achieved by succession investigation of ancient kilns after 1950s, and our ancestors of ceramic made great contributions on the cause, such as Chen Wanli, Feng Xianming, Geng Baochang, Li Huibing, Ye Zhemin, Li Zhiyan, Wang Liying, Ye Peilan, etc. Here we should highly appreciate their hardworking and great contribution.

The ceramic archaeology was a kind of arduous task. Due to the poor conditions in 1950s and no cars available, the experts reached the destination often by tractor, carriage, donkey cart or hiring a bicycle. Sometimes they even went to the kiln site on foot. The experts took the firsthand materials back to the Palace Museum with the condition of severe cold or heat, and sometimes even bite by snake or scorpion, and cut feet and hands were in common. With the persistent pursuit of the objective, our experts overcame every kind of difficulties and collected valuable materials, and made great contribution to the development of our research on ceramic in the Palace Museum.

The period of specimens was from Shang to Qing dynasty, and it reflected the development of Chinese ceramic. The specimens included celadon and black glaze ceramic of Eastern Han, and celadon of Southern and Northern Dynasties; samples of Xing kiln, Ding kiln, Gongxian kiln, Yaozhou kiln, Yue kiln and Changsha kiln in Sui and Tang dynasty; samples of Song dynasty contained Ru kiln, Official kiln, Ding kiln, Jun kiln, Yaozhou kiln, Cizhou kiln, Jingdezhen kiln, Longquan kiln, Yue kiln, and ceramic specimens for export in Fujian and Guangdong, etc.

The specimens contained over 60 thousands pieces involving over 300 kiln sites from 20 different provinces. By variety, there was celadon, white glaze, black glaze, yellow glaze, tricolor, twisted-color glaze, dark reddish brown glaze, green glaze, red and green color, unglazed brown color, blue and white, etc. By type, there was plate, plate with high foot, saucer, bowl, bowl with high foot, cup, basin, jar, vat, censer, vase, pot, pillow, light and box, etc. By decoration, there was incised pattern, cut pattern, engraved pattern, stamped pattern and embossed pattern, etc. Some specimens have been confirmed by wares in excavation and collection, and the others were not common. The specimen materials could make a more clearly understanding about the production of kilns and make up the insufficient of ancient archives and material wares. So the specimens are precious to ceramic study.

The specimens in the collection of the Palace Museum ranked highest in quantity and quality nationwide. Some samples have been exhibited in Britain, Japan and Hongkong, and caused much of a stir worldwide and put forward to the development of study on ceramic. Over the years, the ceramic researchers throughout the country wanted publicity for these specimens in the collection of the Palace Museum, and the public audiences also hoped having a chance to watch the ceramic specimens. In order to satisfied the wishes of special experts and public audiences and construct a platform for the Ancient Ceramic Research Center of the Palace Museum, we will exhibit the specimens comprehensively. At the same time, the series of books will be published, including over 180 kilns and 10,000 specimens. We hope it will reflect the achievement on ceramic research of the Palace Museum and push the forward of the intense research on ancient Chinese ceramic.

故宫博物院陶瓷研究五十五年

李辉柄

瓷器是中国古代的重要发明之一，是对人类文明史做出的杰出贡献。因此，把它作为一门学科进行研究，向来受到国内外学者们的重视。

近代瓷学研究史可划分为两个阶段，一为文献考据阶段，一为考古调查发掘阶段。20世纪50年代以前，学者们主要依据史部与集部有关陶瓷的文献进行考证，诸如《唐六典》、《旧唐书》、《新唐书》、《茶经》、《全唐诗》等典籍，尤其是宋、元以后的陶瓷著录、笔记及方志，如蒋祈的《陶记》、曹昭的《格古要论》、宋应星的《天工开物》、《大清一统志》以及相继出现的《陶说》等专著。因以上研究主要是以文献为基础进行的，即所谓"书斋考古"，所以学者们把它划归为文献考证阶段，该阶段的代表作品是吴仁敬、辛安潮的《中国陶瓷史》。虽然该书在学术上并无独到之处，不能代表当时的最高学术水平，但它毕竟是一部完整的中国陶瓷史。

故宫博物院著名陶瓷学家陈万里先生曾对这本《中国陶瓷史》作过这样的评价："这本书的最大毛病就是采取几个陈旧瓷书里的内容，因袭着以往的传统，作为正确史料，几乎成了一部变相的类书，不是一部陶瓷史。"

陈万里先生是我国第一位走出书斋，运用考古学的方法，对浙江龙泉窑青瓷进行实地古窑废址考察的学者。他认为过去只靠点滴文献史料进行研究的老路是无法取得显著成效的。他自1928年夏，八去龙泉，七访绍兴，搜集了大量瓷片标本，并对它们进行排比研究，开辟了一条瓷器研究的新途径，从而把我国的瓷学研究推进到了一个新的阶段，即考古调查发掘阶段，为现代陶瓷学研究奠定了基础。他撰写的《瓷器与浙江》就是这一阶段的重要代表作。该书可看作是从传统的书斋考古走向古窑遗址考古的一个里程碑性质的著作。

研究瓷器发展的历史，文献史料与实物史料是不可缺少的两个方面。陈万里先生在注重文献史料的同时，对于实物资料也给予充分重视，创造了文献与实物相结合的研究方法。实物资料来源于古瓷窑址与古墓葬发掘两个方面：窑址调查与发掘，目的是为了弄清各窑烧造器物的特征，以便区别窑口（瓷器的烧造地点），正确判断它的窑名；墓葬发掘特别是具有确切纪年的墓葬出土瓷器，可以用来印证古代瓷窑址的时代。陈万里先生从考古学的角度出发，以纪年墓出土物件或是文字记载作为科学依据，与窑址实地考察相印证，从而解决了不少瓷器的窑口与断代问题。

瓷器年代的鉴定与窑口的划分是研究瓷器发展史的基础。故宫博物院的陶瓷研究一直是院内学术研究工作的重点，为了解决陶瓷研究领域中存在的问题，提高陶瓷研究的水平与鉴定能力，从 20 世纪 50 年代开始，就确定了故宫博物院陶瓷研究的基本方针，并制定了长远的研究规划：陶瓷研究的工作分宋代以前与明清两大阶段，既分工又合作，同时进行。宋代以前的瓷器研究以陈万里先生为首组成调查组，对全国南北各地的古代瓷窑遗址进行调查，以解决宋代以前瓷器的窑口即产地问题。明清瓷器的研究则以著名瓷器鉴定专家孙瀛洲先生为带头人组成鉴定组，对故宫博物院藏 32 万多件瓷器，特别是清宫旧藏的明清瓷器进行断代研究，以解决明清瓷器的科学鉴定问题。

魏晋南北朝时期由于社会长期处于分裂割据局面，造成南方与北方青瓷生产与发展的不平衡，故有“南方青瓷”与“北方青瓷”之分。经过调查，南方青瓷的生产主要集中在浙江地区，窑址在浙江的上虞、绍兴、宁波、鄞县、萧山、德清、余杭、永嘉等县市均有发现，其中以上虞最为集中，大部分分布在曹娥江中游两岸，时代均为三国两晋至南朝。

在浙江一带墓葬中出土的南方青瓷极为丰富，以六朝古都南京出土青瓷最多，其中纪年墓葬出土青瓷为数不少，它们反映了不同时期青瓷的发展面貌与特征。绍兴曾发现有“黄龙”、“赤乌”、“永安”、“甘露”、“宝鼎”、“凤凰”、“天册”、“天纪”等年号的三国孙吴时代的墓葬，出土了一些青瓷，其中以刻吴永安三年 (260 年) 铭的青釉谷仓罐最为有名，器物上的纪年为这件器物的断代提供了科学依据。

然而，北方青瓷在中原地区魏晋时期的墓葬里几乎没有发现，北魏迁都洛阳以后的墓葬中，青瓷出土的数量渐多，至北齐时期骤增。最著名的是 1948 年河北省景县发现的北齐封氏墓所出青釉仰覆莲花尊，其造型雄伟、装饰富丽，器身堆贴飞天、兽面、蟠龙、宝相花等纹饰，并浮雕仰覆莲花瓣纹，莲花尊胎厚质坚，青釉润泽，是北方青瓷的代表。

邢窑是见于著录的唐代著名瓷窑之一，但由于长期以来未能发现它的窑址，因而也就始终没有弄清其真实面目。1980 年，首先在河北内丘与临城县交界之地发现了邢窑遗址，但根据唐代李肇《国史补》中“内丘白瓷瓯，端溪紫石砚，天下无贵贱通用之”的记载，邢窑遗址应在内丘，而不是临城。据此，文物工作者又在 1984 年于内丘境内进行调查，果然在 5 个乡方圆 120 公里区域内发现窑址十余处，并采集了大量标本。通过发掘证明了内丘城关一带的唐代瓷窑为当时邢窑瓷器烧制中心，所出白瓷也具备邢窑特征，与《茶经》中“邢磁类银，类雪”的记载相符。内丘城关白瓷窑烧制的器物，往往还在器底部刻划一个“盈”字。西安唐大明宫、唐长安西明寺遗址也曾出土过“盈”字款的碗底残片，与内丘城关邢窑遗址所出相同，应为当时邢窑的贡品。内丘邢窑遗址的发现，证明《国史补》中“内丘白瓷瓯”的记载是准确的，从而解决了中国陶瓷史上一大难题。

文献史料对研究陶瓷发展史也具有重要意义，然而有些文献记载的内容还要运用考古学的方法来加以证实和补充。如文献关于“秘色瓷”的记载，宋人赵德麟的“今之秘色瓷器，世言钱氏有国，越州烧造，为供奉之物，不得臣庶用之，故谓之秘色”。而从唐代陆龟蒙的《秘色越器》诗以及徐寅的《贡余秘色茶盏》诗的记载来看，秘色瓷并非始于五代，在唐代就有秘色之名。由于法门寺塔基出土了一批精致的越窑青瓷，物账单里又把这些青瓷称之为“秘色瓷”，这就有力地证明了越窑青瓷就是当时所谓的“秘色瓷”，从而使长期存在于学术界的这一悬而未决的问题得到了解决。

唐人陆羽《茶经》中记载的越州窑、鼎州窑、婺州窑、岳州窑、寿州窑与洪州窑等唐代六大青瓷窑，除鼎州窑外，其他五个瓷窑的遗址均已发现并进行了重点发掘。这些瓷窑烧瓷的历史以及烧制器物的特征，均与《茶经》记载相符。在全国各个地方志中所记载的瓷窑，有些已经发现，有些还有待考古工作来加以证实。但事实已经证明，通过考古学的方法，既可印证历史文献的内容是否属实，又可弥补有些文献的疏漏之处。

宋代瓷器发展的重要标志就是官窑的建立与民窑的大发展，窑址星罗棋布，遍布于全国各地。构成了宋代瓷器发展的主要特征。

1965 年，经调查首先在河南禹县城北门内的八卦洞发现了烧制宫中用钧窑瓷器的窑址，出土器物的造型、釉色与宫中收藏的钧窑瓷器相同，从而证实了北宋后期曾在禹县建立了官窑。钧窑瓷器完全是根据当时皇室设计式样与宫廷内陈设需要而生产的，器形多为花盆、盆奁、鼓丁洗、出戟尊等，釉色有玫瑰紫、海棠红、月白等，器底刻有一至十的数目字样。

汝窑也属于北宋官窑之一。根据宋代叶寘《坦斋笔衡》中“本朝以定州白瓷器有芒，不堪用，遂命汝州造青瓷器”的记载，汝窑是继定窑之后，为了满足宫廷需要建立起来的官窑。在河南宝丰清凉寺村发现了汝窑遗址，其中所出青瓷工艺之考究，造型之精美，与清宫收藏品完全相同，由此可以确认，河南宝丰清凉寺村即是宋代汝窑的所在地。

杭州乌龟山郊坛下官窑窑址早在 1930 年就已发现，1956 年浙江省文管会对其进行过一次发掘。1985 年冬至 1988 年春，考古工作者又相继对乌龟山窑遗址进行了两次发掘，不仅获得了大量实物标本，而且还揭露出龙窑与作坊等遗迹。

20 世纪 60 年代以来，沿着陈万里先生所开拓的道路前进的著名瓷器研究家冯先铭先生，集录了广博的古代文献和地方志中的陶瓷史料，在陈万里先生考察的基础上，调查了全国各地的古代瓷窑遗址，尤其是对北方的河南、河北、山西、陕西古窑址集中的地区，进行了较深入的考古调查，取得了巨大的成果，基本上弄清了中国古瓷窑的分布及南北重要瓷窑的发展历史与相互关系，为解决各大博物馆藏品的窑口（产地）问题提供了科学依据。冯先铭先生主编的《中国陶瓷史》是继《瓷器与浙江》之后的又一部重要著作。它总结了历代陶瓷的研究成果，代表了这一阶段研究的最高水平，为今后陶瓷史研究的深入发展创造了条件。

宋及宋以前我国瓷窑分布遍及南北各地，瓷器的窑口归属问题是根据古窑址调查发掘来判定的，瓷器的年代是根据墓葬特别是纪年墓葬出土瓷器作为标准器排比出来的。两者相互印证，是解决窑口与判断时代的科学方法。明、清时期，江西景德镇已成为全国的制瓷中心，绝大多数产品均出自景德镇窑。所以，明、清瓷器的鉴定与宋以前的情况不同，它不存在产地即窑口的划分，而只是一个时代的断定。由于已发掘的明、清时期有明确纪年的墓葬很少，出土的瓷器更少，很难作为我们断代的依据，而明、清瓷器也不像唐、宋瓷器那样有较固定的标准，再加上明、清各个具体朝代的年限都不长，瓷器的品种又相当繁杂，后代和前代又存在着一定的连续性，因此，要想做到很精确地断代是困难的。鉴定明、清瓷器的年代，就成为一个主要课题。

20 世纪 50 年代以来，故宫博物院除了以陈万里先生为代表的研究人员在全国开展古窑遗址调查外，还组织院内外专家对清宫旧藏的明、清瓷器进行了一次全面的鉴定。我国著名瓷器鉴定家孙瀛洲先生是采用类型学的方法对明、清带年款的瓷器进行排比研究的第一人。他以明、清带年款的官窑瓷器作为标准器，把不同朝代的瓷器所具有的不同时代特征排比出来，经过研究归纳，得出一些有关鉴定明、清瓷器的科学标准，并把它提到理论化的高度，用以指导实践。在他的指导和参与下，按照上述的科学方法，边排比，边研究，边进行鉴定，把原先对一些瓷器错定了的年代纠正过来，使故宫博物院这项“鉴定工程”得以顺利完成。

随着考古事业的发展与瓷器研究的客观需要，当前我国瓷器研究领域已在前两个阶段的基础上，进入到综合性研究的新阶段。故宫博物院陶瓷研究中心的成立，是这一新阶段的一个重要标志。陶瓷鉴定研究是一门艰辛的学问，尤其是进入现代社会，一些利欲熏心者不惜引进现代科技，仿制和伪造古陶瓷牟取暴利，给陶瓷鉴定带来了新的课题。对此，我们除了要对传统鉴定方法进行科学总结外，还要引进新的科学技术检测手段。在前人研究成果的基础上共同深入研究，不断解决摆在我们面前的疑难问题，把中国的陶瓷研究推向一个更高的水平。

The 55 Years of Research on Ceramic in the Palace Museum

Li Huibing

The ceramic was one of the most important inventions in ancient China, and an outstanding contribution for human culture as well. As an academic discipline, it is widely known by experts in domestic and abroad.

The history of ceramic study in modern times can be generally divided into two stages: one was the method of textual criticism, and another was archaeological investigation and excavation. Before 1950s, the scholars mainly carried out the study by textual research of ancient documents on ceramic. Chen Wanli was the first one to investigate the ancient celadon kilns of Longquan kiln in Zhejiang Province using the method of archaeology. Consequently, our study was put forward to a new level meaning stage of archaeological investigation and excavation. The book of *The Porcelain and Zhejiang Province* was an important representative in the period, and could be regarded as the landmark from scholar' s room to field visit.

The ceramic appreciation on dating and kilns distinction was the basement of ceramic research. In order to solve the problem existed in our study and enhance the level of ceramic research and appreciation. In 1950s, the Palace Museum determined the basic roles on ceramic study and formulated the long-term research program. The work of ceramic research could be divided into two stages: one was before Song dynasty, and another was Ming and Qing dynasty. Under the leadership by Chen Wanli, the work team investigated the ancient kilns all over the country, and tried to judge the specific kiln site of ceramic before Song dynasty. The study of Ming and Qing dynasty was guided by Sun Yingzhou, the famous experts on ceramic. The appreciation team launched the study on over 300 thousands porcelains especially those collected by the Qing Court, and solved the difficult problem of appreciation on Ming and Qing porcelain.

Based on the investigation by Chen Wanli, the famous ceramic expert Feng Xianming successively investigated the ancient kilns all over the country after 1960s, especially in Northern China, such as kilns in Henan, Hebei, Shanxi and Shaanxi Province. The book of *The History of Chinese Ceramic*, which compiled by Feng Xianming, was another famous work after the book of *The Porcelain and Zhejiang Province*. This book reflected the highest level in the period and provided useful materials with study on ceramic history.

The ceramic appreciation on dating and kilns distinction, which belonged before Song dynasty, was mainly judged by kiln investigation and excavation. This is compared to the ceramic appreciation of Ming and Qing dynasty. In this period, Jingdezhen has become the center of ceramic making throughout the country. Due to lack of materials of tombs, the accurate judgment on Ming and Qing ceramic was difficult and became a main study in our work.

For this reason, beside the investigation, the Palace Museum also organized the experts of ceramic to carry out a comprehensive appreciation on Ming and Qing porcelain collected by the Qing Court. According to the method of typology, the famous expert Sun Yingzhou firstly put the porcelain with inscriptions in Ming and Qing dynasty as the standard and analyzed the feature of different period, and then made the conclusion on appreciation criterion. By appreciation criterion, the work went ahead smoothly.

Under the need of development on archaeology and porcelain study, the research has been step into a new stage of comprehensive study. The founding of the Ancient Ceramic Research Center of the Palace Museum became an important landmark in the period. Based on the scholars' achievements, we still need studying deeply to solve the puzzling question and put the research into a new high level.

全国窑址分布图

The Distribution Map of Kilns in China

注：▲窑址

▲故宫博物院已调查的窑址

Notes：▲ Kiln site

▲ Kiln that has been investigated by the Palace Museum

北京

门头沟 ▲
密云 ▲

河北

隆化 ▲
曲阳 ▲
井陉 ▲
临城 ▲
内丘 ▲
邯郸 ▲
彭城 ▲
临水 ▲
磁县 ▲
贾壁 ▲

河南

安阳 ▲
林州 ▲
鹤壁 ▲
浚县 ▲
淇县 ▲
辉县 ▲
焦作 ▲
修武 ▲
新乡 ▲
博爱 ▲
陕县 ▲
新安 ▲
宜阳 ▲
巩义 ▲
荥阳 ▲
密县 ▲
登封 ▲
禹县 ▲
汝州 ▲
宝丰 ▲
郏县 ▲
鲁山 ▲
内乡 ▲
南阳 ▲
邓州 ▲
唐河 ▲

山东

德州 ▲
武城 ▲
临清 ▲
淄博 ▲
淄川 ▲
临淄 ▲
泰安 ▲
宁阳 ▲
泗水 ▲
曲阜 ▲
临沂 ▲
枣庄 ▲

山西

天镇 ▲
大同 ▲
浑源 ▲
广灵 ▲
左云 ▲
怀仁 ▲
朔县 ▲
河曲 ▲
保德 ▲
神池 ▲
代县 ▲
定襄 ▲
静乐 ▲
兴县 ▲
临县 ▲
交城 ▲
文水 ▲
汾阳 ▲
榆次 ▲
孝义 ▲
盂县 ▲
平定 ▲
寿阳 ▲
和顺 ▲
左权 ▲
介休 ▲
灵石 ▲
隰县 ▲
汾西 ▲
霍县 ▲
蒲县 ▲
临汾 ▲
翼城 ▲
乡宁 ▲
浮山 ▲
吉县 ▲
曲沃 ▲
长子 ▲
襄垣 ▲
沁源 ▲
长治 ▲
长子 ▲
壶关 ▲
高平 ▲
阳城 ▲
晋城 ▲
河津 ▲
夏县 ▲

陕西

旬邑 ▲
耀州 ▲
白水 ▲
澄城 ▲
富平 ▲
麟游 ▲

甘肃

武威 ▲
兰州 ▲
华亭 ▲
天水 ▲

内蒙

赤峰 ▲
林东 ▲

宁夏

灵武 ▲

辽宁

辽阳 ▲

安徽

萧县 ▲
淮南 ▲
霍山 ▲
庐江 ▲
繁昌 ▲
枞阳 ▲
泾县 ▲
绩溪 ▲
歙县 ▲
休宁 ▲

江西

景德镇 ▲
乐平 ▲
婺源 ▲
横峰 ▲
弋阳 ▲
铅山 ▲
贵溪 ▲
九江 ▲
靖安 ▲
奉新 ▲
铜鼓 ▲
上高 ▲
丰城 ▲
金溪 ▲
南丰 ▲
广昌 ▲
萍乡 ▲
永丰 ▲
吉安 ▲
宁都 ▲
于都 ▲
赣州 ▲
大余 ▲
寻乌 ▲
定南 ▲
龙南 ▲
全南 ▲

江苏

宜兴 ▲

浙江

长兴 ▲
吴兴 ▲
德清 ▲
余杭 ▲
萧山 ▲
杭州 ▲
临安 ▲
绍兴 ▲
上虞 ▲
诸暨 ▲
嵊县 ▲
宁波 ▲
鄞县 ▲
慈溪 ▲
余姚 ▲
奉化 ▲
象山 ▲
浦江 ▲
义乌 ▲
东阳 ▲
永康 ▲
兰溪 ▲
金华 ▲
武义 ▲
仙居 ▲
临海 ▲
黄岩 ▲
台州 ▲
温岭 ▲
龙游 ▲
衢州 ▲
常山 ▲
江山 ▲
缙云 ▲
丽水 ▲
遂昌 ▲
龙泉 ▲
云和 ▲
庆元 ▲
永嘉 ▲
乐清 ▲
温州 ▲
文成 ▲
瑞安 ▲
泰顺 ▲
苍南 ▲

福建

浦城 ▲
光泽 ▲
崇安 ▲
松溪 ▲
政和 ▲
邵武 ▲
建阳 ▲
建瓯 ▲
顺昌 ▲
南平 ▲
柘荣 ▲
周宁 ▲
福安 ▲
霞浦 ▲
屏南 ▲
宁德 ▲
罗源 ▲
闽侯 ▲
闽清 ▲
福州 ▲
福清 ▲
连江 ▲
泰宁 ▲
建宁 ▲
将口 ▲
宁化 ▲
三明 ▲
大田 ▲
沙县 ▲
长汀 ▲
连城 ▲
永定 ▲
德化 ▲
永春 ▲
安溪 ▲
南安 ▲
同安 ▲
泉州 ▲
晋江 ▲
仙游 ▲
莆田 ▲
厦门 ▲
华安 ▲
长泰 ▲
漳州 ▲
南靖 ▲
龙海 ▲
平和 ▲
漳浦 ▲
云霄 ▲
诏安 ▲
东山 ▲

广东

梅县 ▲
大埔 ▲
五华 ▲
兴宁 ▲
潮州 ▲
饶平 ▲
潮安 ▲
揭阳 ▲
揭西 ▲
揭东 ▲
普宁 ▲
惠来 ▲
海丰 ▲
陆丰 ▲
紫金 ▲
龙川 ▲
惠州 ▲
龙门 ▲
博罗 ▲
惠东 ▲
广州 ▲
乐昌 ▲
仁化 ▲
韶关 ▲
始兴 ▲
乳源 ▲
南雄 ▲
英德 ▲
肇庆 ▲
封开 ▲
高要 ▲
郁南 ▲
佛山 ▲
南海 ▲
三水 ▲
高明 ▲
鹤山 ▲
恩平 ▲
新会 ▲
信宜 ▲
高州 ▲
茂名 ▲
廉江 ▲
遂溪 ▲
吴川 ▲
雷州 ▲
深圳 ▲
澄海 ▲
海康 ▲

海南

澄迈 ▲
东方 ▲
万宁 ▲
陵水 ▲

广西

桂林 ▲
全州 ▲
兴安 ▲
灵川 ▲
临桂 ▲
永福 ▲
钟山 ▲
藤县 ▲
容县 ▲
北流 ▲
柳州 ▲
桂平 ▲
田东 ▲
宾阳 ▲
邕宁 ▲
东兴 ▲
浦北 ▲
合浦 ▲
大新 ▲
百色 ▲

湖北

武昌 ▲
鄂城 ▲

湖南

岳阳 ▲
汨罗 ▲
湘阴 ▲
常德 ▲
益阳 ▲
长沙 ▲
浏阳 ▲
醴陵 ▲
衡阳 ▲
衡东 ▲
衡山 ▲
衡南 ▲
祁东 ▲
耒阳 ▲
常宁 ▲
沅陵 ▲
怀化 ▲
武冈 ▲
新宁 ▲
祁阳 ▲
蓝山 ▲
新田 ▲
道县 ▲
零陵 ▲
郴县 ▲
永兴 ▲
汝城 ▲

四川

广元 ▲
成都 ▲
郫县 ▲
灌县 ▲
大邑 ▲
新津 ▲
彭县 ▲
邛崃 ▲
绵阳 ▲
江油 ▲
乐山 ▲

重庆

南岸 ▲
奉节 ▲

云南

玉溪 ▲
禄丰 ▲
建水 ▲

窑址标本目录

北京

龙泉务窑

山东

淄博窑

曲阜窑

临沂窑

枣庄窑

宁阳窑

陕西

耀州窑

玉华宫遗址

旬邑窑

澄城窑

宁夏

灵武窑

辽宁

辽阳窑

List of Plates

Beijing

Longquanwu Kiln

Shandong Province

Zibo Kiln

Qufu Kiln

Linyi Kiln

Zaozhuang Kiln

Ningyang Kiln

Shaanxi Province

Yaozhou Kiln

The Heritage of Yuhuagong

Xunyi Kiln

Chengcheng Kiln

Ningxia Hui Autonomous Region

Lingwu Kiln

Liaoning Province

Liaoyang Kiln

窑址标本

Plates

北京

北京市目前在密云、门头沟发现窑址。2006年故宫博物院古器物部陶瓷组的研究人员对两处窑址进行了调查。密云小水峪等地的窑址已经很难找到像样的标本，只采集到少量很粗糙的标本，价值不大。龙泉务窑经过考古部门的发掘，窑址标本比较丰富。

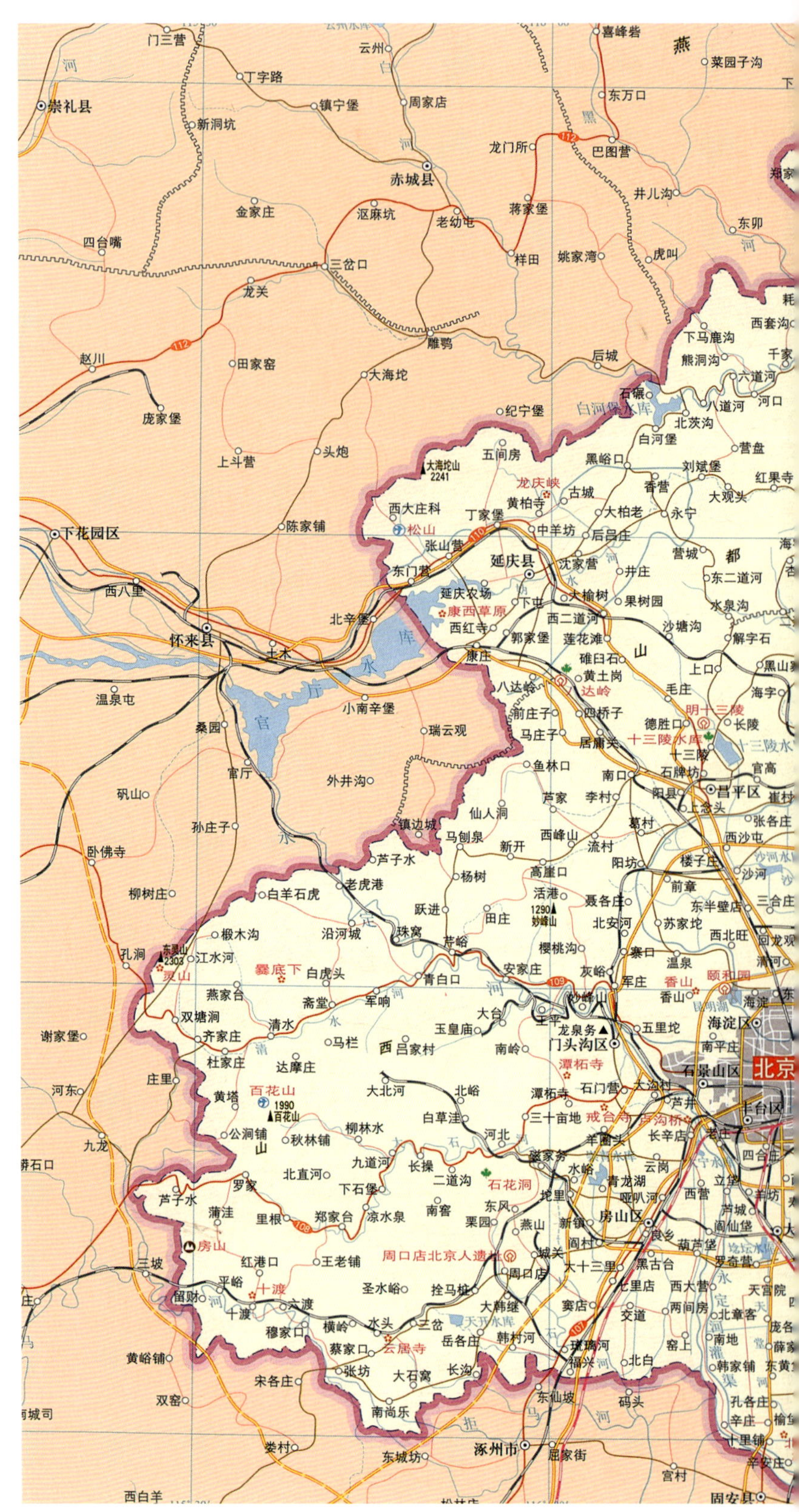

北京窑址分布图

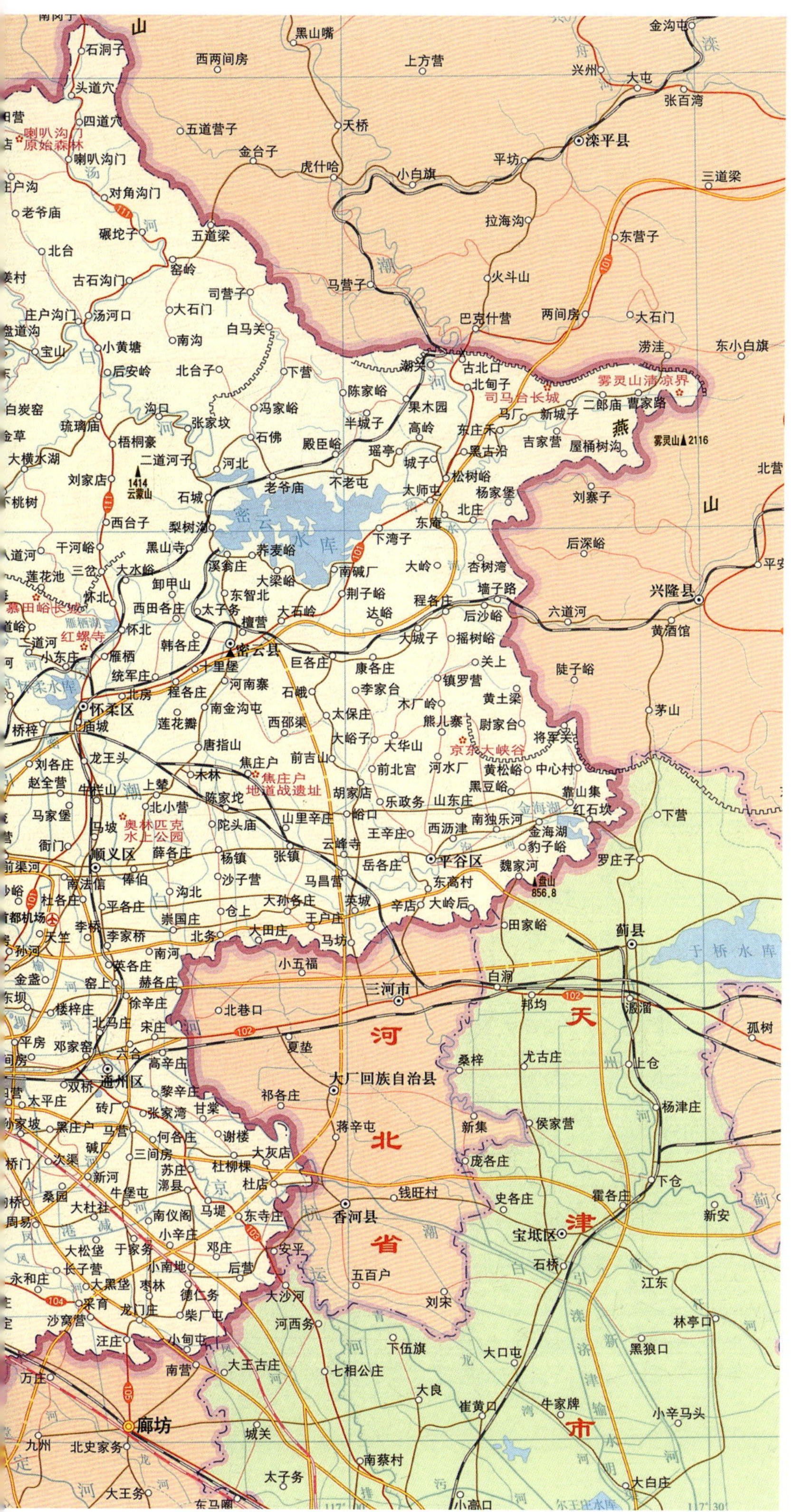

Beijing

The kilns have been discovered only in Mentougou District and Miyun County at present. The researchers from Ceramic Group of Ancient Cultural Relic Department in the Palace Museum investigated the two kiln sites in 2006. The kiln sites in Miyun County were hard to find the decent specimens, so we can only found a few coarse specimens which were unworthy. Since the excavation leading by the related archaeological department, the specimens from kiln site of Longquanwu were relatirely rich.

The Distribution Map of Kilns in Beijing

龙泉务窑

2006年故宫博物院古器物部陶瓷组研究人员对龙泉务窑遗址进行了调查。龙泉务窑为辽代瓷窑，窑址在北京市门头沟区龙泉务村。20世纪50年代发现，90年代北京市文物研究所有关人员对窑址进行了考古发掘。发掘成果表明，龙泉务窑创烧于辽代早期，衰落于金代初期，是北方地区一处有代表性的辽金制瓷窑址。主要以烧造白釉瓷器为主，兼烧青釉、黑釉瓷器。器物有粗、细之分。造型以各式碗、盘、碟、罐等为主，钵、枕、炉、盒、执壶等也占有一定比重。白釉器物受河北定窑的一些影响，其中部分器物如葵口盘、折腰盘、浮雕莲瓣纹壶等与河北定窑、山西地区某些仿定窑的瓷器风格接近，在装饰上也模仿定窑的莲瓣纹等装饰。与定窑相比，龙泉务窑白釉器物大多数没有定窑器物胎质致密，显得有些疏松；白釉呈粉白色，不似定窑的白釉白中泛黄，光泽感较好；支烧工艺有所不同，定窑采用正烧或覆烧，盘、碗里心不留叠烧的痕迹，而龙泉务窑盘、碗等里心或足部因叠烧多留有三至四个支烧痕，而四支钉这种支烧方法在其他地区瓷窑如唐代安徽寿州窑，金代山东淄博窑、山西浑源窑以及辽代赤峰缸瓦窑等一些瓷窑使用。

Longquanwu Kiln

The researchers of Ceramic Group of Ancient Cultural Relic Department in the Palace Museum investigated the Longquanwu kiln in 2006. The kiln site of Longquanwu was located at Longquanwu Village of Mentougou District in Beijing. As a kiln of Liao dynasty, the Longquanwu kiln mainly fired the white glaze ware and some celadon ware and black glaze in the minority. The firing technology in Longquanwu kiln was affected by the Ding kiln in Hebei to a certain degree. The white glaze ware could be categorized into fine one and rough one, and some has the similar style comparing to the Ding kiln and kilns in Shanxi area such as sunfloral-shaped rim plate, waisted plate and pot with lotus design. Compared with the white glaze ware of Ding kiln, the white ware of Longquanwu kiln has the following characters: coarse body other than fine one, pink white glaze other than yellowish white with shiny look, 3 to 4 spur-marks at inner bottom or foot of bowl and plate other than without any trace of spur-marks because of the firing technology. The firing method of exited spur-marks was only found in Shouzhou kiln of Anhui in Tang dynasty, Hunyuan kiln of Shanxi in Jin dynasty, and Gangwa kiln of Chifeng in Liao dynasty, etc.

龙泉务窑遗址
The heritage of Longquanwu kiln

龙泉务窑遗址
The heritage of Longquanwu kiln

1 辽 白釉瓶标本

Liao dynasty

Specimens of white glaze vase

2 辽　白釉瓶标本

Liao dynasty

Specimens of white glaze vase

3 **辽 白釉瓶标本**

Liao dynasty

Specimens of white glaze vase

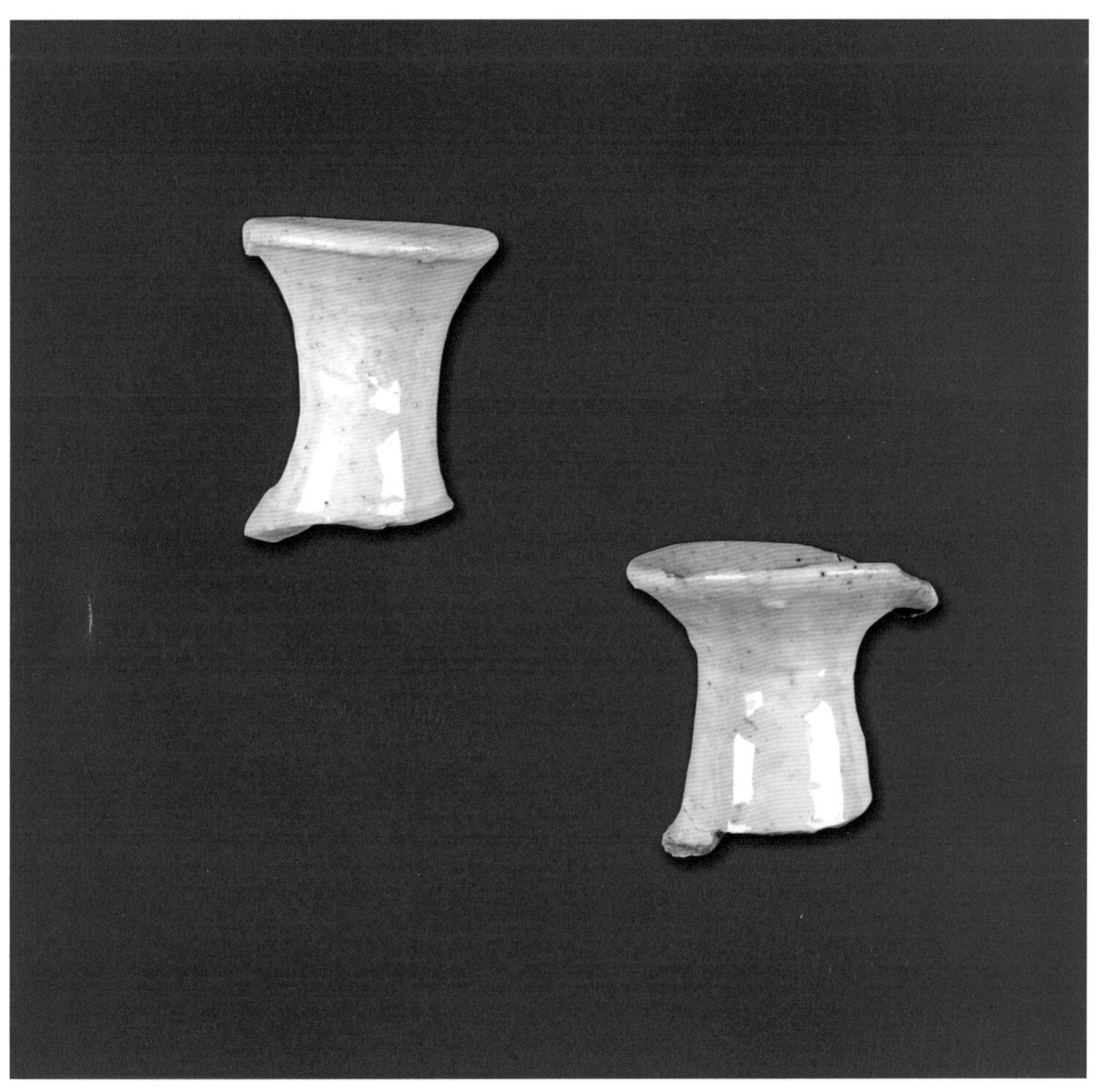

4 **辽　白釉折肩罐标本**

Liao dynasty

Specimens of white glaze jar with oblique shoulder

附图

辽　白釉刻花折肩罐

高 12.6 厘米　口径 9.8 厘米
足径 7.7 厘米
北京市龙泉务窑遗址出土
北京市文物研究所藏

Illustration
Liao dynasty　White glaze jar with oblique shoulder and carved design

Height 12.6cm, mouth diameter 9.8cm, foot diameter 7.7cm
Excavated at Longquanwu kiln of Beijing and collection of the Cultrual Relic Research Institution of Beijing

罐直口，短颈，折肩，深腹，圈足。通体施白釉，釉面莹润，外壁剔刻变形蕉叶纹。

此式折肩罐是龙泉务窑的典型器形，造型规整，胎细釉润，刻花纹饰刀工洗练，是辽代晚期龙泉务窑细白瓷的代表作。

5　辽　白釉罐标本

Liao dynasty

Specimens of white glaze jar

6 辽 白釉执壶标本

Liao dynasty

Specimen of white glaze pot with handle

附图

辽 白釉刻花执壶

高 11.4 厘米 足径 6 厘米
北京市龙泉务窑遗址出土
北京市文物研究所藏

Illustration

Liao dynasty White glaze pot with handle and carved design

Height 11.4cm, foot diameter 6cm
Excavated at Longquanwu kiln of Beijing and collection of the Cultrual Relic Research Institution of Beijing

执壶小口，短颈，折肩，鼓腹，圈足。肩部一侧出短流，另一侧饰双条形曲柄，附平顶带宝珠钮盖。胎质细腻，胎色洁白。通体施白釉，釉面润泽。外壁刻花装饰，肩饰一周菊瓣纹，腹饰间隔排列的蕉叶纹和仰莲纹。

执壶是龙泉务窑最具特色的一种器物造型，壶体一般不大，高度在11厘米左右，器形多为折肩直流曲柄，腹部筒形或瓜棱形。此件执壶为龙泉务窑辽代晚期产品，造型秀巧，分层刻花纹饰清晰精美。

7 辽 白釉枕标本
Liao dynasty
Specimen of white glaze pillow

8 辽 白釉钵缸标本
Liao dynasty
Specimens of white glaze vat

9 辽 白釉碗标本

Liao dynasty

Specimens of white glaze bowl

10 **辽　白釉碗标本**

Liao dynasty

Specimens of white glaze bowl

11 **辽 白釉花口碗标本**

Liao dynasty

Specimens of white glaze bowl with flower-shaped edge

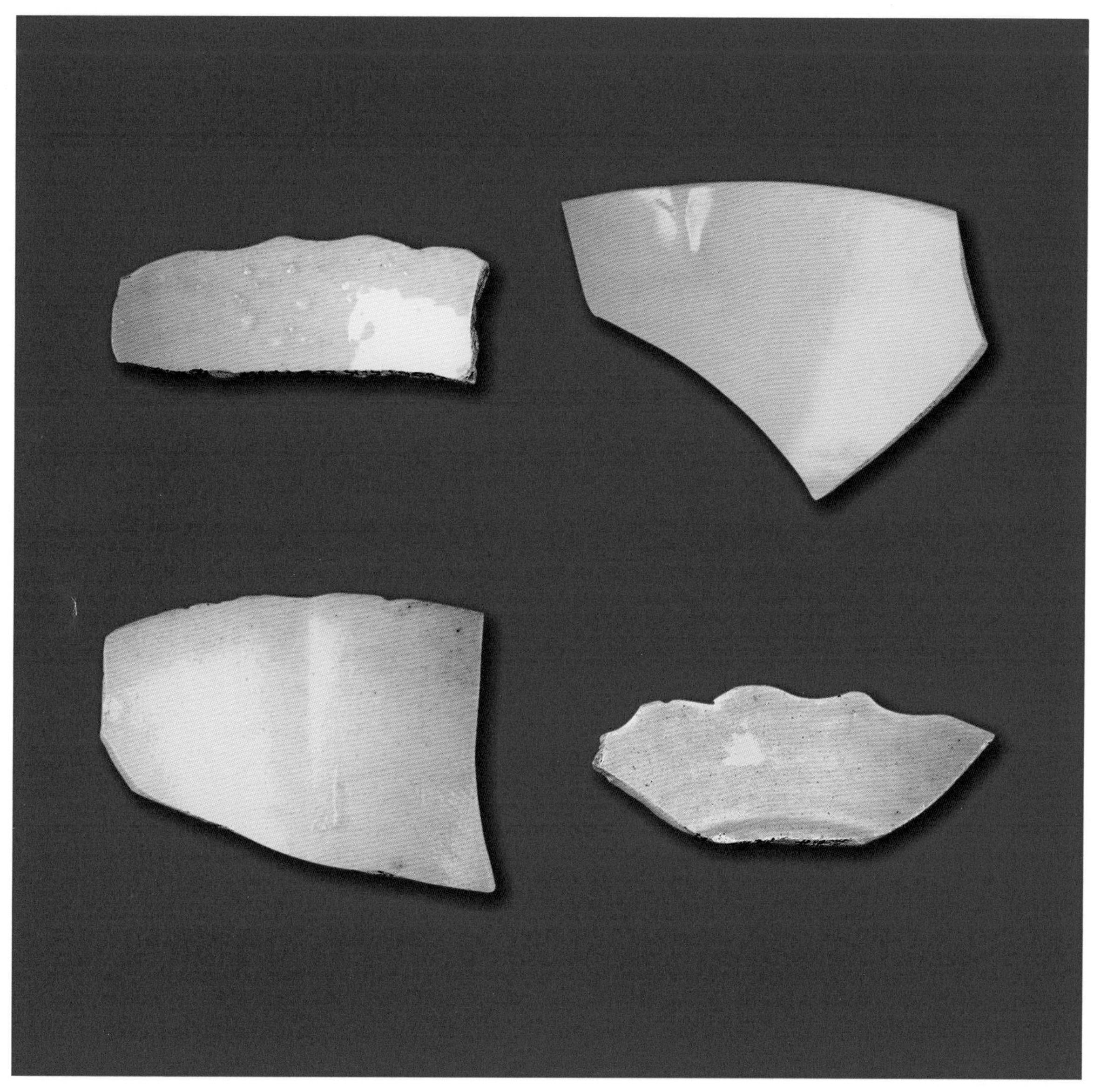

12 辽 白釉折沿盘标本

Liao dynasty

Specimens of white glaze plate with flatted edge

附图

辽 白釉点褐彩花式折沿盘

高 6.5 厘米 口径 24.8 厘米
足径 9.2 厘米
北京市龙泉务窑遗址出土
北京市文物研究所藏

Illustration
Liao dynasty White plate with flatted edge and brown color

Height 6.5cm, mouth diameter 24.8cm, foot diameter 9.2cm
Excavated at Longquanwu kiln of Beijing and collection of the Cultrual Relic Research Institution of Beijing

盘折沿，呈六出荷叶形，弧壁，圈足。胎质细腻坚致，胎色洁白。通体施白釉，釉面莹润，釉色白中泛青。

此盘仿同时期金银器造型，六曲花瓣形的花式和盘壁出棱颇似宋代流行的银质锤鍱器物，而盘里心及花式内凹处点褐彩装饰，和盘心遗留的四处窄长支钉痕，是辽代晚期龙泉务窑盘类器的典型特征。

13 辽 里白釉外黑釉碗标本

Liao dynasty

Specimens of bowl with white glaze inside and black glaze outside

14　辽　里白釉外酱釉碗标本
Liao dynasty　Specimens of bowl with white glaze inside and dark reddish brown glaze outside

15　辽　黑釉罐标本

Liao dynasty

Specimens of black glaze jar

16　**辽　黑釉器盖标本**
Liao dynasty
Specimen of black glaze cover

17　**辽　黑釉枕标本**
Liao dynasty
Specimen of black glaze pillow

18　**辽　黄釉瓶标本**
Liao dynasty
Specimen of yellow glaze vase

19　辽　素胎哨标本

Liao dynasty

Specimens of unglazed whistle

山东

山东省目前已在淄博、曲阜、临沂、枣庄、宁阳等地发现古窑址。故宫博物院部分陶瓷专家和学者于20世纪70年代调查了淄博磁村窑、博山窑后，又于2000年、2006年对淄博磁村窑、寨里窑、巩家务窑进行了调查，同时还调查了曲阜宋家村窑、何家店窑、息陬窑，临沂窑，枣庄窑，宁阳窑等窑址。

山东省早期窑址以淄博寨里窑为代表，有北朝到隋的青釉标本。北朝时期的青釉莲花尊标本在此地有少量发现，因此此地有可能是莲花尊的产地，但有待进一步调查。隋、唐时期曲阜、宁阳等窑址的发现，丰富了学界对山东地区早期窑址的认识。金、元时期瓷窑集中在淄博与枣庄等地，主要烧制白釉、白釉划花、黑釉、白地黑花器物，淄博窑以黑釉凸线纹装饰的器物最具代表性。近些年又在山东地区发现了绞胎器物，与河南地区的绞胎器物在釉色、器形上均不相同。目前对山东地区古窑址的调查还很薄弱，有待进一步深入。

山东窑址分布图

Shandong Province

The ancient kilns have been discovered in Shandong Province including Zibo, Qufu, Linyi, Zangzhuang and Ningyang at least for now. After the investigation on Cicun kiln and Boshan kiln in 1970s, the ceramic experts and scholars of the Palace Museum took the further reseatch of the kilns of Shandong Province in 2000 and 2006, including Songjiacun kiln in Qufu, Hejiadian kiln, Xizou kiln, Linyi kiln, Zaozhuang kiln and Ningyang kiln etc.

As one of the important representative of ancient kilns in Shandong Province, the Zhaili kiln in Zibo produced the celadon specimens from Northern Dynasties to Sui dynasty. It was the possible producing area for celadon Zun with lotus design, since the founding of the specimens in Sui dynasty. The discovery of Qufu kiln and Ningxiang kiln enriched the acquaintance on early kilns in Shandong Province by scholars. The main products of kilns in Zibo and Zaozhuang which belongs to Jin and Yuan dynasties included white glaze, white glaze incised design, black glaze and black color on white ground, etc, and ware of black ware with outstanding string design was the most representative variety in Zibo kiln. The twisted colored wares have been founded in Shandong Province in recent years, but those were different from wares of Henan Province in glaze and type. The investigation of kilns in Shandong Province was still insufficient which needs to make a thorough study.

The Distribution Map of Kilns in Shandong Province

淄博窑

故宫博物院的专家和学者于20世纪70年代调查了淄博磁村窑、博山窑遗址后，又于2000年、2006年对该窑磁村、寨里、巩家务窑遗址进行了调查。

磁村窑，窑址在山东省淄博市西南10公里的磁村。1976年被重点发掘，出土物表明磁村窑始于唐而终于元，有600年的历史。唐代以烧黑釉为主，宋代改烧白瓷，装饰有剔花、划花，白釉胎质较粗厚，碗口径较大，有的装饰绿彩。此外还发现了绞胎、白地黑花（彩绘、点彩）、红绿彩绘、三彩等品种。金元时期除烧白瓷外，黑釉占有一定比例。与北方其他瓷窑一样，在烧瓷品种上也受到磁州窑的一定影响。较有特色的装饰是黑釉凸线纹，盛行于金代，在光亮的釉质上线纹清晰，有些罐的双系下方，饰有斜十字纹，比较独特。此类装饰的器物在河北、河南、四川等地瓷窑均有烧造。

博山窑，窑址在山东省淄博市博山县。主要烧制青釉印花碗等器物。标本中的青褐釉印花碗，与山西地区仿定窑黑釉印花产品相似，但胎质较为粗糙。纹饰多为缠枝花卉，有牡丹、菊花等纹。碗心多有一圈涩圈，金代风格明显。

寨里窑，窑址在山东省淄博市寨里村。窑址遗存较少，有北朝到隋代及宋代遗物。北朝到隋代烧青釉瓷器，从采集的标本来看，胎质较粗，有青釉碗、高足盘等，宋代有黑釉碗。

巩家务窑，窑址位于山东省淄川岭子镇巩家务村。该窑址还不为更多的人所知。在窑址采集到白釉、黑釉、酱釉瓷器标本。白釉有罐、碗，碗的数量最多，里心有三四个较大的支烧痕。还有白釉剔花，白釉点彩品种；黑釉有罐、碗、小杯、碟等；还烧制黑褐釉小动物雕塑，有人骑马、鱼、小马等，造型丰富，形象可爱。

Zibo Kiln

The ceramic experts and scholars of the Palace Museum investigated the kilns of Cicun and Boshan in 1970s and 2000, then the kilns of Cicun, Zhaili and Gongjiawu in 2006 successively.

The kiln site of Cicun is located at Cicun village which is 10 kilometers far from the southwest Zibo, Shandong Province. It could be put the conclusion that the Cicun kiln which started firing from Tang to Yuan dynasty has a history over 600 years based on the excavation in 1976. Comparing to the black glaze ware in Tang dynasty, the Cicun kiln produced white glaze ware which was decorated with incised design in Song dynasty. The white glaze bowl has large mouth diameter, coarse body, and some decorated with green color. In that period, the new varieties also included twisted colored, black color on white ground, red and green color, tricolor, etc. In Jin and Yuan dynasty, the black glaze ware also occupied a certain proportion except of white one in Cicun kiln. The kiln was influenced by Cizhou kiln in variety as other kilns in northern area, and ware of black ware with outstanding string design was the most representative variety in Jin dynasty. The ware has the character of fine type, glossy glaze and distinct pattern, some even decorated with unique inclined cross design. This kind of ware was also fired at kilns in Hebei, Henan and Sichuan Province.

The kiln site of Boshan was located at Boshan County in Zibo, Shandong Province. The main product of Boshan kiln was celadon bowl with stamped design which has coarse body, and was similar to black glaze bowl with stamped design in Shanxi area. The popular design of the kiln was entwined floral including peony, chrysanthemum, etc. The inner bottom of most bowls had a circle of trace without glaze which clearly represented the style of Jin dynasty.

The kiln site of Zhaili is located at Zhaili Village in Zibo, Shandong Province. The heritages of kiln which belong to Northern Dynasties, Sui dynasty and Northern Song dynasty were retained less comparatively. Based on the specimens, the Zhaili kiln produced celadon including bowl and plate with high foot from Northern Dynasties to Sui dynasty, and black glaze bowl in Northern Song dynasty.

The kiln of Gongjiawu is located at Gongjiawu Village in Lingzi Town, Zichuan, Shandong Province. The specimens included wares of white glaze, black glaze and dark reddish brown glaze. There were jars and bowls of white glaze, and bowl with 3 or 4 spur-marks at inner bottom was the mainstream. Besides, white glaze with incised design and white glaze with colors became the new varieties. The kiln produced jars, bowls, cups and saucers of black glaze, and even lovely animal sculptures including horsemen, fish, horse, etc.

淄博磁村窑窑址保护碑
The stele of kiln protection in Cicun kiln, Zibo

淄博磁村窑遗址
The heritage of Cicun kiln in Zibo

20　**北朝至隋　青釉碗标本**
From Northem Dynasties to Sui dynasty
Specimens of celadon bowl

21　唐　黑釉葫芦瓶标本
Tang dynasty　Specimen of black glaze vase in shape of calabash

22　唐　黑釉罐标本
Tang dynasty
Specimen of black glaze jar

23　唐　黑釉壶标本
Tang dynasty
Specimens of black glaze pot

24　唐　黑釉碗标本

Tang dynasty

Specimens of black glaze bowl

25　唐　黑釉碗标本

Tang dynasty

Specimens of black glaze bowl

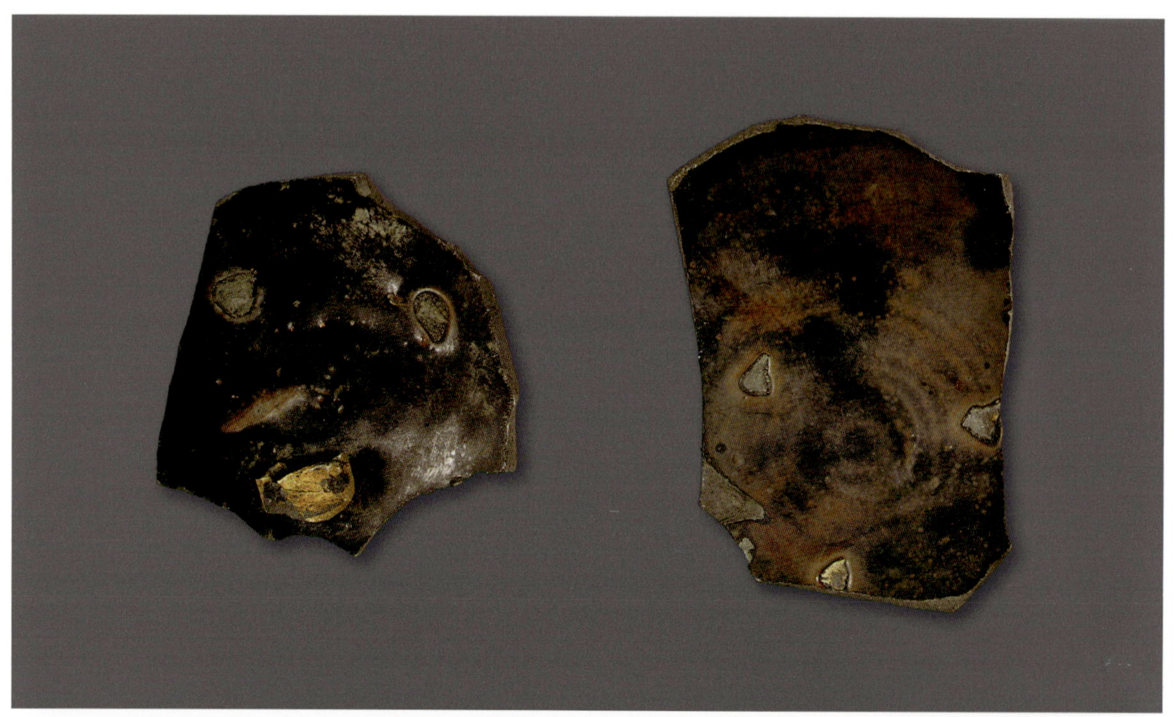

26　唐至五代　白釉绿彩碗标本

From Tang dynasty to Five Dynasties

Specimens of white glaze bowl with green color

27　唐至五代　里茶叶末釉外酱釉碗标本

From Tang dynasty to Five Dynasties

Specimen of bowl with tea-dust glaze inside and dark reddish brown glaze outside

28 宋（金） 白釉双系罐标本

Song dynasty (Jin dynasty)

Specimen of white glaze jar with two handles

附图

宋 白釉双系罐

高 6.5 厘米 口径 8.2 厘米
足径 5.7 厘米
故宫博物院藏

Illustration
Song dynasty
White glaze jar with two handles

Height 6.5cm, mouth diameter 8.2cm,
foot diameter 5.7cm
Collection of the Palace Museum

罐直口，短颈，颈、腹间置对称环形耳，腹略鼓，腹下渐收，近底处外撇，宽圈足内凹。通体施白釉，外壁施釉不到底，釉面有细碎纹片。

此种造型常见于河北、河南、山东等北方窑口。

29　宋（金）　白釉炉标本
Song dynasty (Jin dynasty)
Specimen of white glaze incense burner

30　宋（金）　白釉碗标本
Song dynasty (Jin dynasty)
Specimen of white glaze bowl

31　宋（金）　白釉刻花碗标本
Song dynasty (Jin dynasty)
Specimen of white glaze bowl with carved design

32 宋（金） 白釉划花碗标本

Song dynasty (Jin dynasty)

Specimens of white glaze bowl with incised design

33　宋（金）　白釉剔花罐标本
Song dynasty (Jin dynasty)
Specimen of white glaze jar with engraved design

34　宋（金）　白釉剔花罐盖标本
Song dynasty (Jin dynasty)
Specimens of white glaze jar cover with engraved design

35　宋（金）　黑白釉铃标本
Song dynasty (Jin dynasty)
Specimen of black and white glaze bell

36 宋（金） 里白釉外黑釉碗标本

Song dynasty (Jin dynasty)

Specimens of bowl with white glaze inside and black glaze outside

37 宋（金） 黑釉瓶标本
Song dynasty (Jin dynasty)
Specimen of black glaze vase

38 宋（金） 黑釉炉标本
Song dynasty (Jin dynasty)
Specimen of black glaze incense burner

39 宋（金） 黑釉碗标本
Song dynasty (Jin dynasty)
Specimen of black glaze bowl

40　**宋（金）　黑釉盏托标本**
Song dynasty (Jin dynasty)
Specimen of black glaze saucer

41　**宋（金）　黑釉贴花罐标本**
Song dynasty (Jin dynasty) Specimen of black glaze jar with applied floral design

42　**宋（金）　黑釉酱彩双系罐标本**
Song dynasty (Jin dynasty)
Specimen of black glaze jar with two handles and dark reddish brown color

43　宋（金）　黑褐釉双系罐标本
Song dynasty (Jin dynasty)
Specimen of light black glaze jar with two handles

44　宋（金）　褐釉双系罐标本
Song dynasty (Jin dynasty)
Specimen of brown glaze jar with two handles

45　宋（金）　褐釉跳刀纹双系罐标本
Song dynasty (Jin dynasty)
Specimen of brown jar with two handles and carved spots design

46 宋（金） 酱釉碗标本

Song dynasty (Jin dynasty)

Specimen of dark reddish brown glaze bowl

47 金 黑釉凸线纹双系罐标本

Jin dynasty

Specimen of black glaze jar with two handles and outstanding string design

附图

金 黑釉凸线纹双系罐

高 11.7 厘米　口径 9.8 厘米
足径 6.8 厘米
故宫博物院藏

Illustration

Jin dynasty　Black glaze jar with two handles and outstanding string design

Height 11.7cm, mouth diameter 9.8cm, foot diameter 6.8cm
Collection of the Palace Museum

罐敞口，短颈，颈、腹间置对称环形耳，垂腹，腹下渐收，宽圈足内凹外撇。胎色黄中泛微红，胎质粗糙。通体施黑釉，外壁施釉不到底。腹部凸起黄褐色线纹四组。素底无釉。

宋金时期，在河南、河北、山东等地的瓷窑中黑釉瓶、罐等瓷器常以凸起的棱线作装饰，又称“出筋”，多数为黑釉白条纹，亦有黑釉褐条纹。布局可分为单线、复线、多线几种，使单调的釉面呈现变化之美。山东淄博窑凸线纹与河北等地同类器物不同，在漆黑光亮的釉面线纹凸起，很有立体感。

48 金 黑釉凸线纹罐标本

Jin dynasty

Specimens of black glaze jar with outstanding string design

附图

金　黑釉凸线纹罐

高 11.4 厘米　口径 8.6 厘米
足径 7 厘米
故宫博物院藏

Illustration
Jin dynasty　Black glaze jar with outstanding string design

Height 11.4cm, mouth diameter 8.6cm , foot diameter 7cm
Collection of the Palace Museum

罐直口，短颈，溜肩，肩以下渐收，近底处外撇，圈足。通体施黑釉，口沿一周无釉，外壁施釉不到底，有流釉现象。腹部凸起黄褐色线纹。素底无釉。

此罐造型小巧，凸起的线条起到了明显的装饰作用，别具一格。

49　金　黑釉凸线纹罐标本
Jin dynasty Specimens of black glaze jar with outstanding string design

50 **金 酱釉碗标本**
Jin dynasty
Specimen of dark reddish brown glaze bowl

51 **金至元 白地黑花罐标本**
From Jin to Yuan dynasty
Specimens of white glaze jar with black color design

52　**金至元　白地黑花盆标本**

From Jin to Yuan dynasty

Specimens of white glaze basin with black color design

53　金至元　白地黑花盆标本

From Jin to Yuan dynasty

Specimens of white glaze basin with black color design

54 宋至元 窑具标本

From Song to Yuan dynasty

Specimens of kiln furniture

55 金 酱釉印花花卉纹碗标本

Jin dynasty Specimen of dark reddish brown glaze bowl with stamped floral decoration

56　金　酱釉印花花卉纹碗标本

Jin dynasty　Specimens of dark reddish brown glaze bowl with stamped floral decoration

淄博寨里窑遗址
The heritage of Zhaili kiln in Zibo

淄博寨里窑遗址
The heritage of Zhaili kiln in Zibo

57 北朝 青釉碗标本
Northern Dynasties
Specimens of celadon bowl

58 北朝 青釉垫柱
Northern Dynasties
Specimen of celadon kiln furniture

淄博巩家务窑遗址
The heritage of Gongjiawu kiln in Zibo

淄博巩家务窑遗址瓷片遗存
The porcelain shred accumulation of Gongjiawu kiln in Zibo

59　宋（金）　白釉双系罐标本
Song dynasty (Jin dynasty)
Specimens of white glaze jar with two handles

60　宋（金）　白釉罐标本
Song dynasty (Jin dynasty)
Specimen of white glaze jar

61　**宋（金）　白釉瓜棱罐标本**

Song dynasty (Jin dynasty)

Specimen of white glaze melon-shaped jar

62　**宋（金）　白釉灯标本**

Song dynasty (Jin dynasty)

Specimen of white glaze light

63 宋（金） 白釉碗标本

Song dynasty (Jin dynasty)

Specimens of white glaze bowl

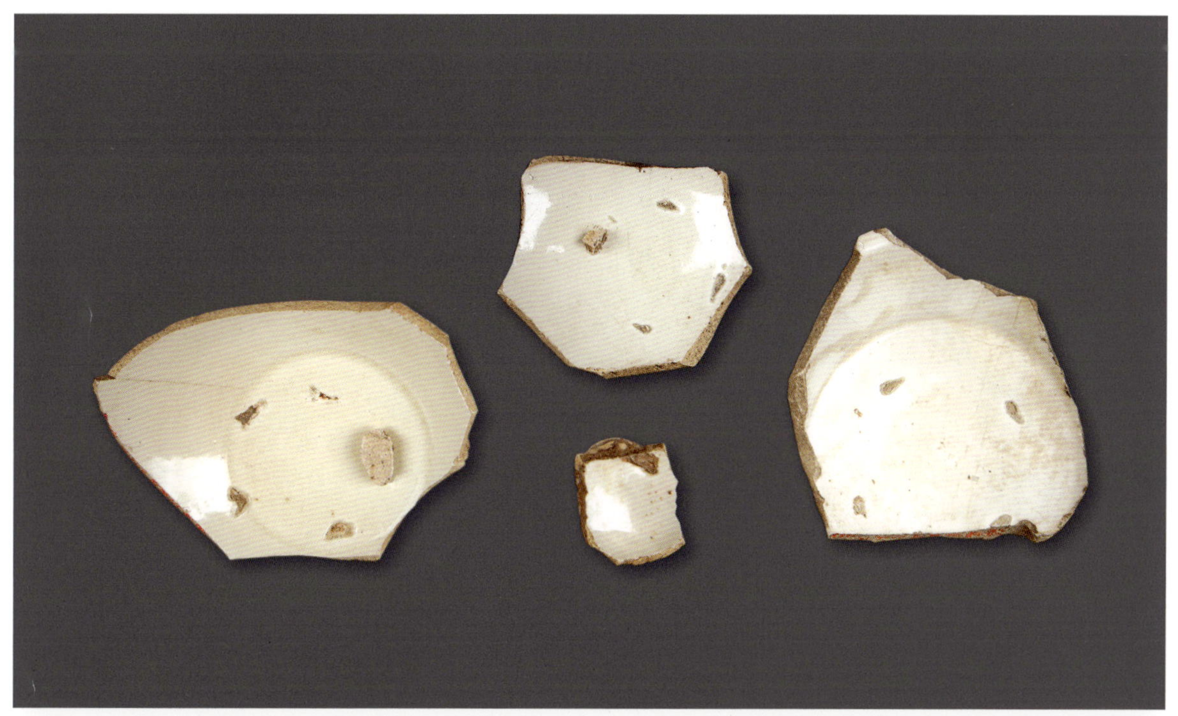

64　宋（金）　白釉剔花器盖标本
Song dynasty (Jin dynasty)
Specimen of white glaze cover with engraved design

65　宋（金）　黑釉瓶标本
Song dynasty (Jin dynasty)
Specimens of black glaze vase

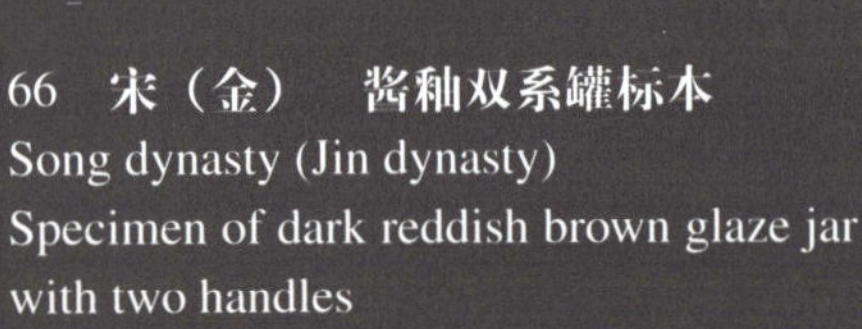

66　宋（金）　酱釉双系罐标本
Song dynasty (Jin dynasty)
Specimen of dark reddish brown glaze jar with two handles

67　宋（金）　酱釉碗标本
Song dynasty (Jin dynasty)
Specimen of dark reddish brown glaze bowl

68
宋（金）　酱釉凸线纹罐标本
Song dynasty (Jin dynasty)
Specimen of black glaze jar with outstanding string design

69　宋（金）　酱釉印花花卉纹碗标本

Song dynasty (Jin dynasty)

Specimens of dark reddish brown glaze bowl with stamped floral design

70　宋（金）　绿釉瓶标本

Song dynasty (Jin dynasty)

Specimen of green glaze vase

71　**宋（金）　窑具标本**

Song dynasty (Jin dynasty)

Specimens of kiln furniture

曲阜窑

曲阜窑是 2006 年故宫博物院专家学者调查山东地区重点瓷窑之一。主要调查了曲阜的宋家村、何家店、息陬等处古窑址，均为隋到宋金时期瓷窑。

宋家村窑，窑址位于曲阜市东南方向 10 公里处，20 世纪 70 年代被发现。该窑隋代烧青瓷器，采集有隋青釉碗、杯、罐、盒等标本，玻璃质感强，有的开片，有垂釉现象，部分胎色上有火石红色。其中小盖盒，胎质细腻，造型小巧，在隋代器物中比较少见。

何家店窑，窑址位于曲阜正北 20 多公里的董庄乡何家庄村。窑址分布在路边农田高台上，在树林及农田里，采集到隋代青釉器标本及宋金时期白釉、黑釉器标本以及垫圈、三叉支钉等窑具。

息陬窑，窑址位于曲阜市东南方向，在村边，尚存窑址保护碑。在田间沟边采集到隋代青瓷与宋金瓷片以及三叉形窑具。

Qufu Kiln

The Qufu kiln, which investigated by the ceramic experts and scholars of the Palace Museum in 2006, was one of the most important kilns in Shandong Province. The main investigation subjects were the kiln of Songjiacun, Hejiazhuang and Xizou, and all belonged to the time from Sui to Jin dynasty.

Songjiacun kiln which was found in 1970s is located at 10km far from southeast Qufu. Based on the specimens collected at the kiln site, the kiln produced celadon of Sui dynasty including bowl, cup, jar, box, etc. The specimens had the following features: glassiness glaze, crackle in glaze, dropping glaze, body with red trace because of firing. The covered box which has fine body and exquisite type was rare in Sui dynasty.

The Hejiadian kiln site is located at Hejiazhuang Village, Dongzhuang Town which was 20km far from north Qufu. The kiln site generaly often distributed at stage of farmland and woods. The specimens included celadon wares of Sui dynasty, black glaze and white glaze wares of Song and Jin dynasty, also some kiln tools such as circle for firing, three-pronged spur-marks, etc.

Xizou kiln is located at southeast of Qufu. The kiln protection stele was still existed near the village. The specimens included celadon ware of Sui dynasty, porcelain samples and three-pronged spur-marks of Song and Jin dynasty which were collected at farmland.

曲阜宋家村窑窑址保护碑
The stele of kiln protection in Songjiacun, Qufu

曲阜宋家村窑瓷片遗存
The porcelain shred accumulation of Songjiacun kiln in Qufu

72　隋　青釉罐标本
Sui dynasty
Specimen of celadon jar

73　隋　青釉碗标本
Sui dynasty
Specimens of celadon bowl

74　隋　青釉碗标本

Sui dynasty

Specimens of celadon bowl

75 隋 窑具标本

Sui dynasty

Specimens of kiln furniture

76　隋　窑具标本
Sui dynasty
Specimens of kiln furniture

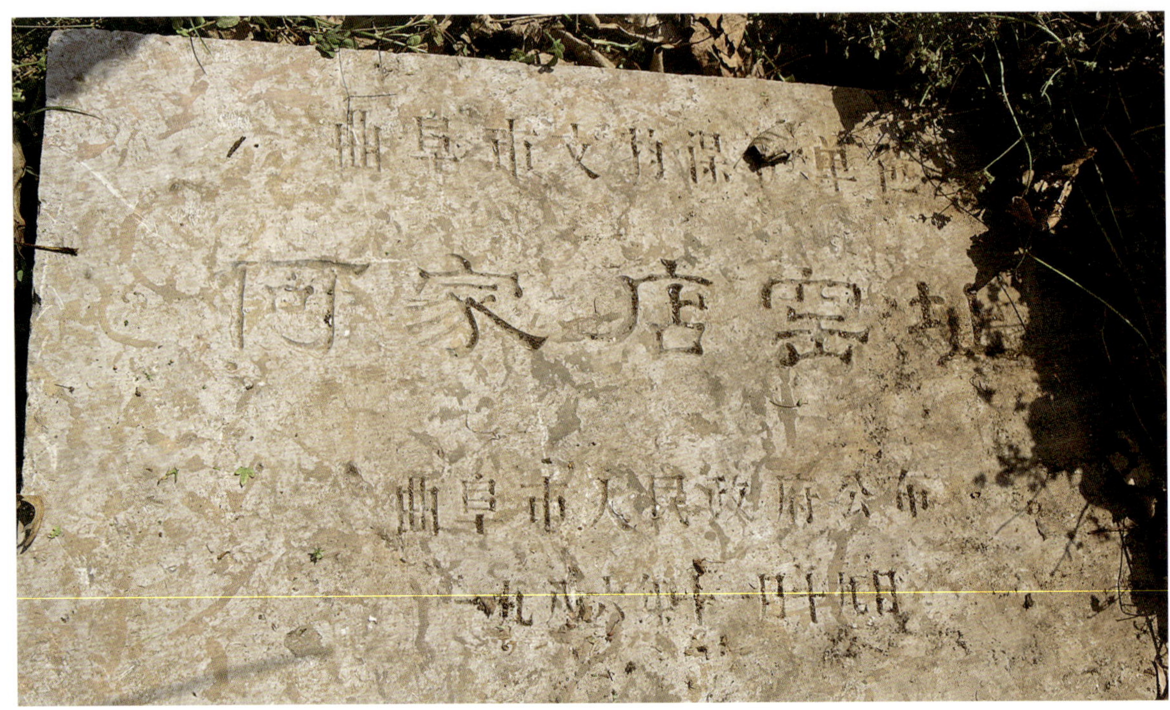

曲阜何家店窑遗址保护碑
The stele of kiln protection in Hejiadian kiln, Qufu

曲阜何家店窑遗址
The heritage of Hejiadian kiln in Qufu

77　金　白釉碗标本

Jin dynasty

Specimens of white glaze bowl

78　金　白釉碗标本

Jin dynasty

Specimen of white glaze bowl

79　金　白釉盆标本

Jin dynasty

Specimen of white glaze basin

曲阜息陬窑遗址保护碑
The stele of kiln protection in Xizou kiln, Qufu

曲阜息陬窑遗址
The heritage of Xizou kiln in Qufu

80　隋　青釉碗标本

Sui dynasty

Specimens of celadon bowl

81 隋 青釉碗标本

Sui dynasty

Specimens of celadon bowl

82 **隋　青釉碗标本**
Sui dynasty
Specimens of celadon bowl

83 **隋　青釉盆标本**
Sui dynasty
Specimen of celadon basin

84　唐　白釉碗标本
Tang dynasty
Specimens of white glaze bowl

临沂窑

故宫博物院部分专家学者于2006年对该窑进行了调查。该窑窑址在临沂朱陈龙泉寺公园内，保存状况不乐观，只河岸附近有极少的宋金时期标本，临沂窑始烧于唐，宋、金为其盛烧期。主要烧造白釉、黑釉、酱釉器物。碗类多采用刮圈叠烧，碗里心都留有涩圈。早年临沂博物馆工作人员调查该窑发现的早期青釉器标本如唐代青黄釉碗、罐等没有找到。

Linyi Kiln

The Zhuchen kiln is located at Longquan Park in Linyi, and the ceramic experts and scholars of the Palace Museum investigated the kiln in 2006. The condition of the kiln protection could not make us be optimistic. Only a few specimens of Song and Jin dynasty can be founded near the riverbank, and wares of white glaze, black glaze and dark reddish glaze were the main product, but samples of Tang dynasty such as yellowish green glaze bowl and jar mentioned by staffs of Linyi Museum based on early investigation were not discovered.

临沂窑遗址
The heritage of Linyi kiln

临沂窑遗址
The heritage of Linyi kiln

85 宋（金） 白釉碗标本
Song dynasty (Jin dynasty)
Specimen of white glaze bowl

86 宋（金） 黑釉瓶标本
Song dynasty (Jin dynasty)
Specimen of black glaze vase

87 宋（金） 黑釉碗标本
Song dynasty (Jin dynasty)
Specimens of black glaze bowl

88 宋（金） 黑釉碗标本

Song dynasty (Jin dynasty)

Specimens of black glaze bowl

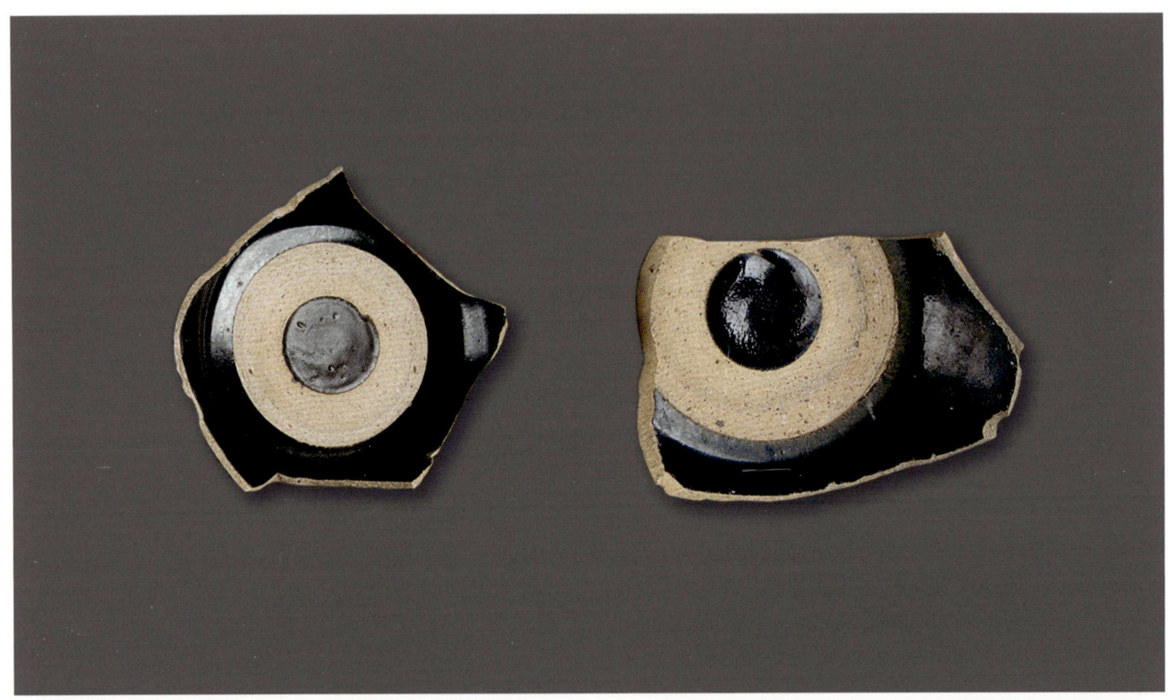

89 宋（金） 酱釉双系罐标本

Song dynasty (Jin dynasty)

Specimen of dark reddish brown glaze jar with two handles

90 宋（金） 酱釉罐标本

Song dynasty (Jin dynasty)

Specimens of dark reddish brown glaze jar

枣庄窑

窑址位于山东省枣庄市薛城区邹坞镇蟠龙河畔的中陈郝村，创烧于北朝晚期，盛烧于金、元，衰落于清末，是山东地区烧造历史延续时间最长，制瓷产量大，生产品种十分丰富的一处民间瓷窑。1987 年曾被山东大学考古系师生发掘，故宫博物院部分专家学者于 2006 年对该窑进行了调查。该窑内涵比较丰富，在方圆 5 公里范围内，村北部主要为青瓷区，南部为白瓷（白地黑花）区、西部为黑瓷区。主要采集到北朝到隋青釉碗、瓶、罐、高足盘等器物标本；唐黄釉、褐釉碗标本。宋、金时期窑址范围较大，主要烧制白釉、白地黑花、黑釉等北方地区常见瓷器品种。此窑还烧制动物小玩具，还有不少窑柱、三叉支钉、工形支具等窑具。

Zaozhuang Kiln

The kiln site is located at Zhongchenhao Village in Zouwu Town, Xuecheng Distrcit. The archaeology department of Shandong University excavated the kiln in 1987, and the ceramic experts and scholars of the Palace Museum investigated the kiln in 2006. The kiln heritages which cover an area over 5km included celadon, white glaze (black color on white ground), black glaze, etc. The porcelain samples collected in this kiln were celadon bowl, vase, jar and plate with high foot in Sui dynasty, yellow glaze and black glaze bowl of Tang dynasty. The widely kiln site of Song and Jin dynasty produced popular varieties in northern area such as white glaze, black color on white ground, white glaze, etc. Besides, the kiln even produced the animal-shaped toy, and kiln furniture like kiln column and so on.

枣庄（中陈郝）窑遗址保护碑

The stele of kiln protection in Zhongchenhao kiln, Zaozhuang

枣庄窑遗址

The heritage of Zaozhuang kiln

91 **北朝至隋　青釉双系罐标本**
From Northern Dynasties to Sui dynasty
Specimens of celadon jar with two handles

92　**北朝至隋　青釉罐标本**
From Northern Dynasties to Sui dynasty
Specimens of celadon jar

93　**北朝至隋　青釉缸标本**
From Northern Dynasties to Sui dynasty
Specimen of celadon vat

94 北朝至隋　青釉碗标本

From Northern Dynasties to Sui dynasty
Specimens of celadon bowl

95 北朝至隋　青釉碗标本

From Northern Dynasties to Sui dynasty
Specimens of celadon bowl

96　北朝至隋　青釉高足盘标本

From Northern Dynasties to Sui dynasty

Specimens of celadon plate with high foot

97　隋　青釉罐标本

Sui dynasty

Specimen of celadon jar

98　隋　青釉碗标本

Sui Dynasty

Specimens of celadon bowl

99 隋 青釉碗标本

Sui Dynasty

Specimens of celadon bowl

100 隋 青釉划花水波纹碗标本

Sui Dynasty

Specimen of celadon bowl with incised ripple design

101 隋至唐 青釉碗标本

From Northern Dynasties to Sui dynasty

Specimens of celadon bowl

102 宋（金） 白釉双系罐标本

Song dynasty (Jin dynasty)

Specimen of white glaze jar with two handles

附图

金 白釉双系罐

高 24.2 厘米 口径 18.3 厘米
足径 10.5 厘米
1987 年枣庄窑遗址出土
枣庄市博物馆藏

Illustration
Jin dynasty White glaze jar with two handles

Height 24.2cm, mouth diameter 18.3cm, foot diameter 10.5cm
Excavated at Zaozhuang kiln in 1987 and collection of the Zaozhuang Museum

罐敛口，短颈，溜肩，肩部饰对称条形双系，鼓腹，圈足。施白釉，里满釉，外半截釉并有点状绿彩装饰。

金、元时期，枣庄窑受河北磁州窑的影响，主要生产磁州窑类型的白釉、白地黑花、白釉绿彩等瓷器品种。此罐即为这一时期的典型器物。与磁州窑同类造型相比，枣庄窑的罐式造型肥矮，溜肩，鼓腹，腹的最大径往往在腹部中间或偏下，口下有弦纹，口呈宽唇状。磁州窑器形较高，为直口，短颈，宽肩，肩以下斜收至底，其腹部的最大径在肩部或上腹部。

103　宋（金）　白釉罐标本
Song dynasty (Jin dynasty)
Specimens of white glaze jar

104　宋（金）　白釉罐盖标本
Song dynasty (Jin dynasty)
Specimen of white glaze jar cover

105　宋（金）　白釉碗标本
Song dynasty (Jin dynasty)
Specimen of white glaze bowl

106 宋（金） 白釉碗标本

Song dynasty (Jin dynasty)

Specimens of white glaze bowl

107 宋（金） 白地黑花瓶标本

Song dynasty (Jin dynasty)

Specimen of white glaze vase with black color design

附图

金至元 白地黑花四系瓶

高 28.1 厘米 口径 5 厘米

足径 8.5 厘米

1987 年枣庄窑遗址出土

枣庄市博物馆藏

Illustration

From Jin to Yuan dynasty

White glaze vase with black color design and four handles

Height 28.1cm, mouth diameter 5cm, foot diameter 8.5cm

Excavated at Zaozhuang kiln in 1987 and collection of the Zaozhuang Museum

瓶撇口，短束颈，溜肩，肩部饰四条形系，长弧腹，圈足。外壁上部施白釉并饰黑彩弦纹和简笔花卉纹，下部施黑釉。

此瓶是枣庄窑所产磁州窑类型白地黑花瓷中的代表作，与磁州窑同类器相比，两色釉间的分界线多为斜线，显得比较随意；条形系上下宽窄差别不大。磁州窑两色釉间的分界线一般平行于器身，显得十分齐整；条形系多上宽下窄略呈倒三角形。

108
宋（金）　白地黑花瓶标本
Song dynasty (Jin dynasty)
Specimen of white glaze vase with black color design

109
宋（金）　白地黑花罐标本
Song dynasty (Jin dynasty)
Specimen of white glaze jar with black color design

110 宋（金） 白地黑花罐标本

Song dynasty (Jin dynasty)

Specimen of white glaze jar with black color design

附图

金至元 白地黑花花卉纹双系罐

高 21 厘米 口径 15.4 厘米

足径 10.5 厘米

1987 年枣庄窑遗址出土

枣庄市博物馆藏

Illustration

From Jin to Yuan dynasty

White glaze jar with black color floral design and two handles

Height 21cm, mouth diameter 15.4cm, foot diameter 10.5cm

Excavated at Zaozhuang kiln in 1987 and collection of the Zaozhuang Museum

罐敞口，短颈，溜肩，肩饰双系，鼓腹，圈足。里满施白釉，外壁上部施白釉饰黑彩弦纹和折枝花卉纹，下部施黑釉。

此罐造型曲线秀美，胎质细腻，釉面莹润，纹饰绘画笔意洒脱流畅，与磁州窑同类产品相比，除造型有所区别外，画工随意，腹部中间主题纹饰超出罐腹上下的弦纹线，不如磁州窑器的画工工整规矩。

111 宋（金） 白地黑花罐标本

Song dynasty (Jin dynasty)

Specimens of white glaze jar with black color design

112 宋（金） 白地黑花盆标本
Song dynasty (Jin dynasty)
Specimen of white glaze basin with black color design

113 宋（金） 黑釉壶标本
Song dynasty (Jin dynasty)
Specimen of black glaze pot

114 宋（金） 黑釉盘标本
Song dynasty (Jin dynasty)
Specimens of black glaze plate

宁阳窑

窑址位于宁阳县以东 35 公里的磁窑镇，省级文物保护单位。故宫博物院部分专家学者于 2006 年对该窑进行了调查。窑址保护面积 1500×500 米，有隋、唐、五代、宋代遗存。采集到隋唐时期青釉、白釉、黄釉器物标本，器形以碗为主，多为厚胎平底，青釉釉色浅青，地方色彩浓郁，多采用支钉叠烧，里心留有三个支烧痕，足有平底、玉璧底、环足等几种。由于该处窑址未遭破坏，标本质量较好。宋代标本有白釉、黑釉器，白釉与北方其他地区风格近似，其工艺也是先施白色化妆土，再施透明釉。双系罐的造型与枣庄窑比较接近。碗多采用支钉支烧，里心及足边留有三四个支烧痕。

Ningyang Kiln

As a cultural relic under provincial-level protection, the kiln site is located at Ciyao Town which is 35km far form eastern Ningyang County, and was investigated by the ceramic experts and scholars of the Palace Museum investigated the kiln in 2006. The area of kiln site covers 1500×500m including the heritages of Sui, Tang, Five Dynasties and Song dynasty. The collected specimens included celadon, white glaze and yellow glaze of Sui and Tang dynasty. As the mainstream product, the bowl has the following features: light celadon glaze, thick body, flat bottom, 3 spur-marks at inner bottom, and some even had foot such as flat foot, ring foot, etc. Since the kiln was untouched before. The porcelain samples like black glaze and white glaze belong to Song dynasty, The white one which covered engobe under clear glaze has the similar style and technology with other kilns in northern areas.

宁阳窑遗址
The heritage of Ningyang kiln

宁阳窑遗址瓷片遗存
The porcelain shred accumulation of Ningyang kiln

115　隋至唐　青釉碗标本

From Sui to Tang dynasty

Specimens of celadon bowl

116 唐 青釉碗标本

Tang dynasty

Specimens of celadon bowl

117 **唐　青釉碗标本**

Tang dynasty

Specimens of celadon bowl

118　**唐　白釉碗标本**

Tang dynasty

Specimens of white glaze bowl

119 **唐至五代　白釉碗标本**

From Tang dynasty to Five Dynasties

Specimen of white glaze bowl

120

宋（金）　白釉双系罐标本

Song dynasty (Jin dynasty)

Specimen of white glaze jar with two handles

121

宋（金）　白釉罐标本

Song dynasty (Jin dynasty)

Specimens of white glaze jar

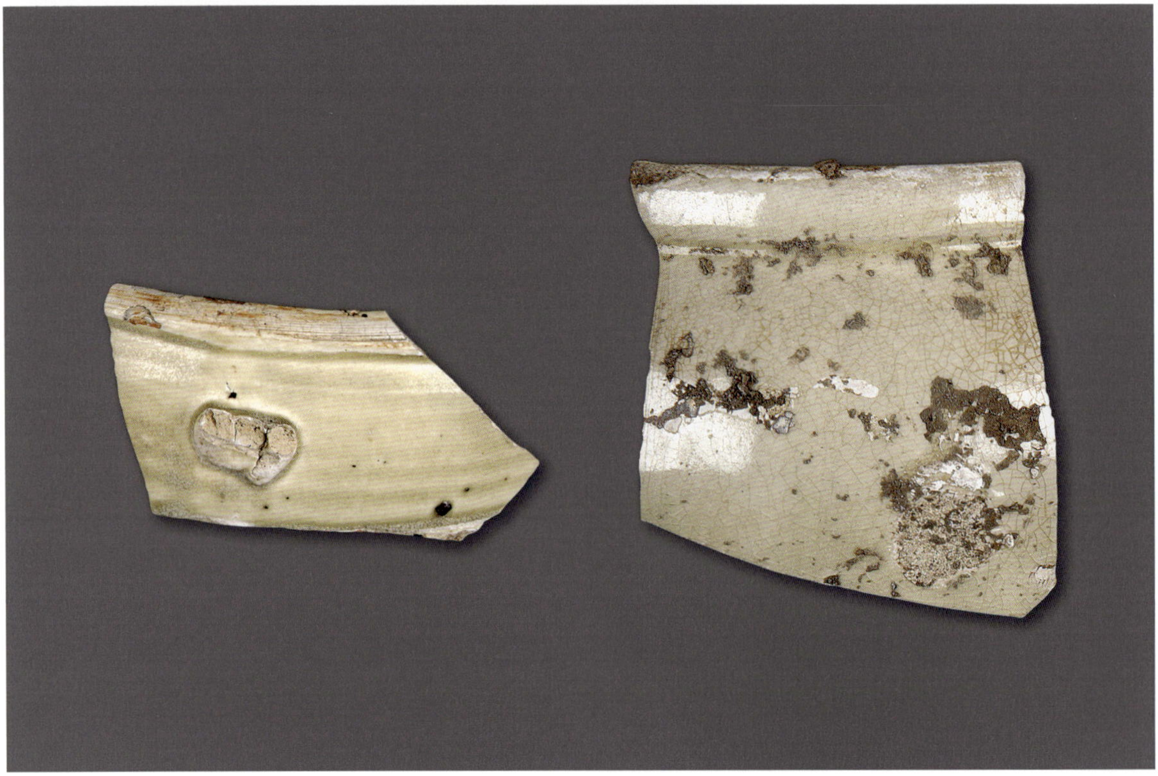

122　宋（金）　白釉碗标本
Song dynasty (Jin dynasty)
Specimens of white glaze bowl

陕西

陕西省古窑址发现数量不多，主要有耀州窑、旬邑窑、澄城窑。故宫博物院部分专家学者于 1954 年、1957 年、1975 年、1977 年、1986 年、2006 年 6 次调查铜川耀州窑遗址，发现从宋到清的六座有关烧造的窑神庙碑及唐青釉、黑釉、酱釉、素胎黑釉、白釉绿彩标本。1959 年陕西省考古所对黄堡镇耀州窑进行了重点发掘，揭露面积 1200 多平方米，发现了唐、宋、金、元不同时期文化层，有作坊和窑炉等遗迹，出土标本 8 万多片。铜川耀州窑的发掘为北宋瓷器分期和宋金两代瓷器的划分找到了依据，是 1949 年以来瓷窑遗址发掘取得成绩最大的一个。2006 年文物考古工作者又对旬邑窑、澄城窑进行了较为详细地调查，取得了一些成绩。

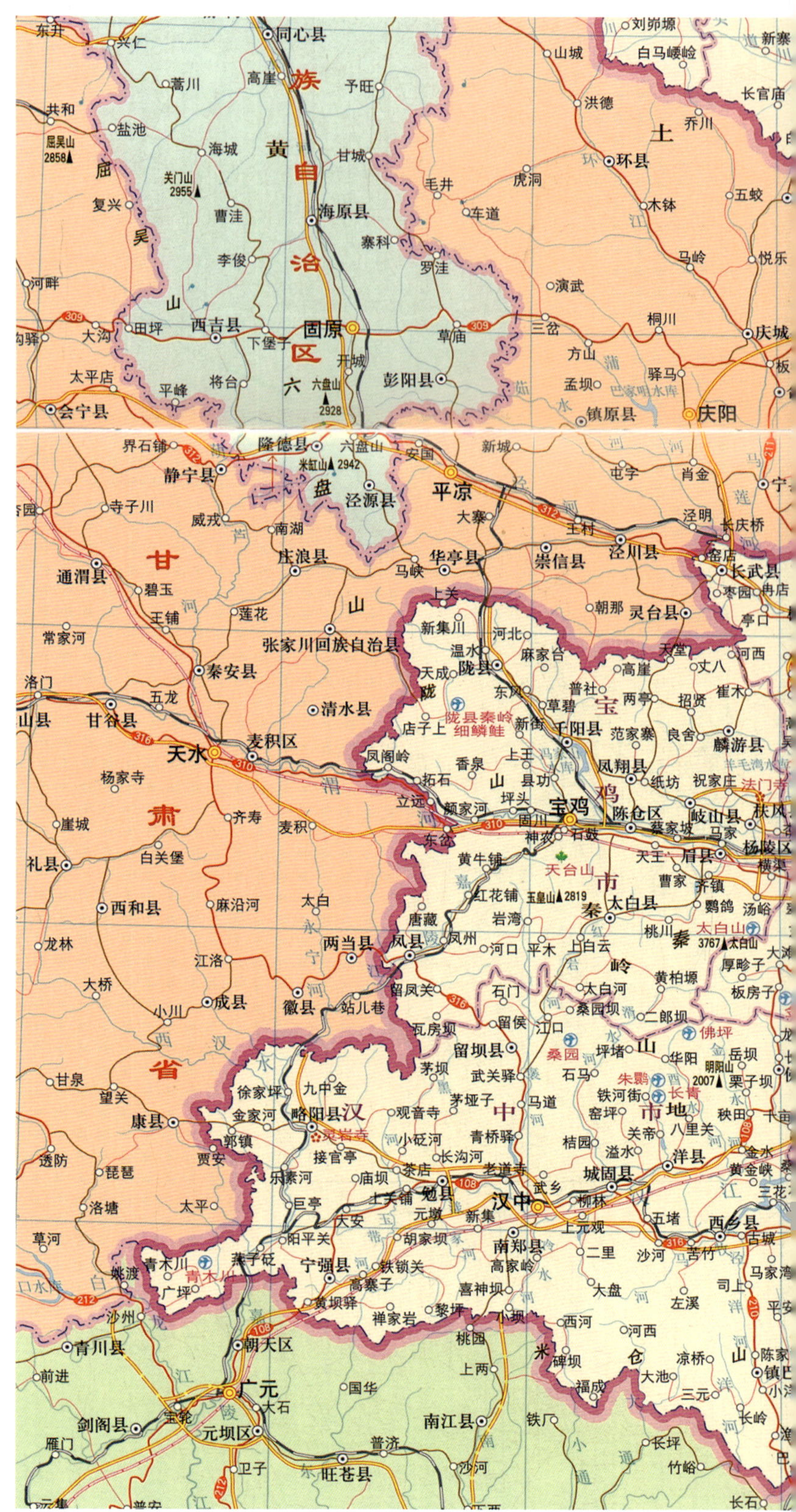

陕西窑址分布图

Shaanxi Province

There were a few kilns discovered in Shaanxi Province. The ceramic experts and scholars of the Palace Museum investigated the Yaozhou kiln in 1954, 1957, 1975, 1977, 1986 and 2006, and found the specimens of Tang dynasty and 6 steles for the Temple of Kiln God from Song to Qing dynasty. In 1959, the Archaeology Intuition of Shaanxi Province excavated Yaozhou kiln in Huangpu Town. The heritages, which cover an area of 1200 square meters, were discovered over 80000 specimens, workshops and kiln furnace belonging to different cultural layer such as Tang, Song, Jin and Yuan dynasty. The excavation of Yaozhou kiln provided the basis with the porcelain of Northern Song dynasty by stages and division of porcelain in Song and Jin dynasty, and was the most significant achievements in excavation of kiln after 1949. The workers of cultural relic and archaeology inquired the kilns detailedly and discovered some ancient kilns in recent years.

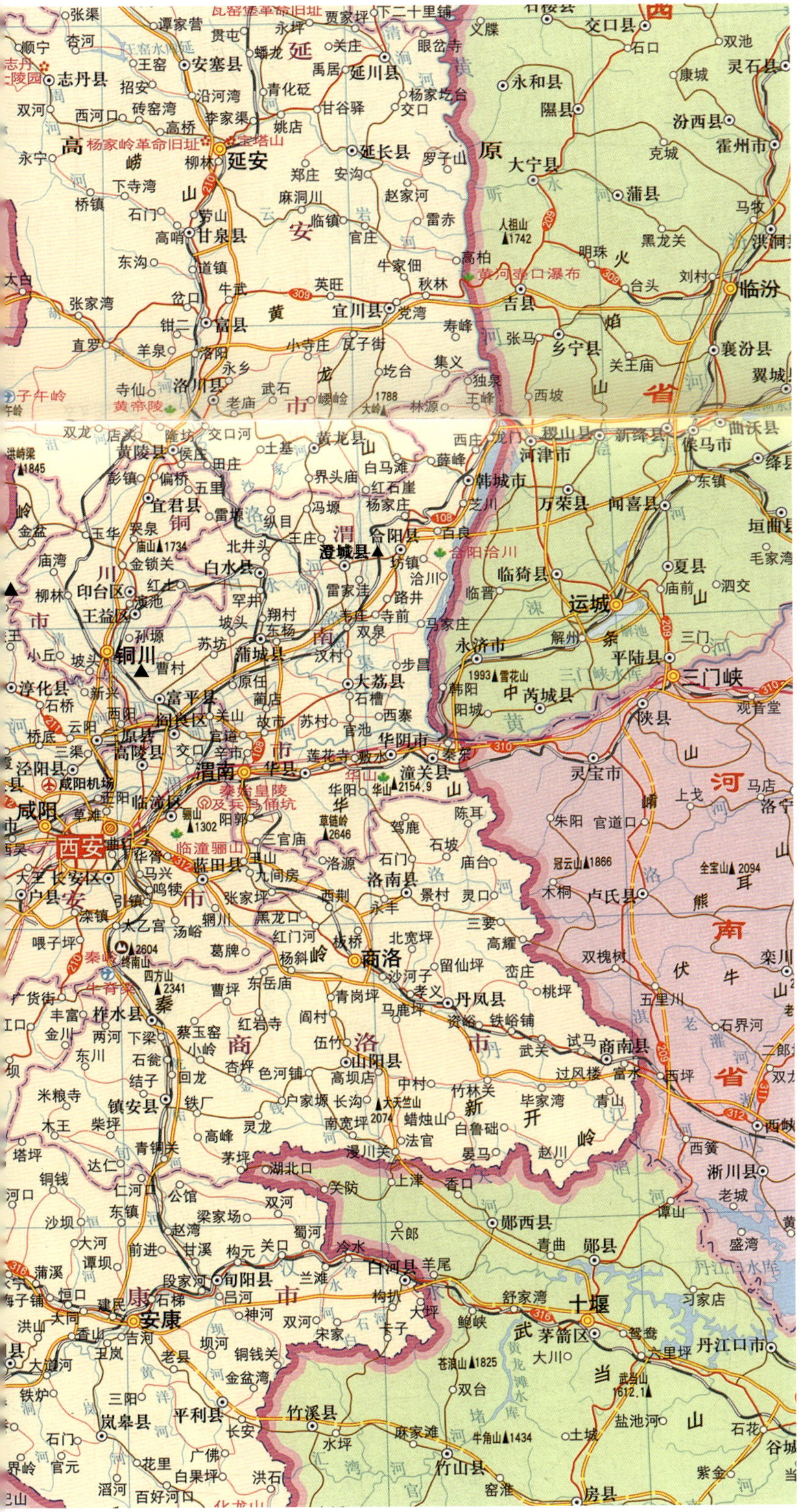

The Distribution Map of Kilns in Shaanxi Province

耀州窑

20世纪50年代、70年代、80年代，2006年，故宫博物院的部分专家学者对耀州窑黄堡镇、陈炉窑址进行了调查。耀州窑位于陕西省铜川市，1954年发现，窑址主要分布在黄堡镇、陈炉、立地坡、上店等地，以黄堡镇遗址面积最大，为20世纪50年代故宫博物院专家调查窑址收获最大的瓷窑。

耀州窑创烧于唐，终于元，北宋为极盛时期，对邻近地区瓷窑有较大的影响，形成了一个以耀州窑为中心的瓷窑体系。

唐代有白釉、黑釉、黄釉、青釉及素胎黑花等品种。黑釉最多，白釉次之，青釉最少。青的色调为青黄、灰绿及褐黄，釉层很薄，胎深灰色。器形有碗、瓶、壶等，碗多为玉璧底，里心多有三个支烧痕，与河南唐代瓷窑具同一特征。瓶类器皿多平底，施半釉。从上述情况可明显看出青釉还处于初创阶段。黑釉有壶、瓶、罐、盆、盘、盒等，釉质较青釉为佳。在盘心、盒盖上用黑釉描绘纹饰，比较特殊，在素胎上以黑釉原料点画，此种装饰以往从未见过，可以说是一个新发现。

五代烧制青釉、浅青釉、月白釉等器物。青釉碗满釉裹足支烧，有刻“官”字者，有细线划花者。特别是近些年出土了一批釉色浅青，近乎青白釉的碗、花式碗、盏托、双鱼瓶、莲瓣尊、莲瓣碗、刻花壶等，造型精致，胎釉细润，有的专家认为是“柴窑”。

宋代以烧青釉为主，并烧少量酱釉器物，刻花出现最早，中期以后刻、划并用，印花装饰开始出现，晚期印花上升为主要装饰。耀州窑刻花为宋代刻花瓷器之最，刀法犀利，纹饰精美，具有很强的立体感。

北宋中期耀州窑为官府选中，烧制供宫廷使用的瓷器，纹饰以龙凤纹为主，与民间用瓷有明显区别。1953年北京广安门外出土了大量耀州窑龙凤纹盘、碗残片，曾推断其为耀州窑贡瓷，后来在窑址发掘中找到龙纹大盘碎片，佐证了推论，王存《元丰九域志》中耀州贡瓷器五十事的记载也有了实物依据，可以互相印证。

黄堡镇金代文化层出土有“大安二年”铭文瓷片和“正隆通宝”铜钱，出土瓷器与北宋有明显不同，碗里心因采用叠烧，多刮去一圈釉，为我们留下了一个断代的重要依据。碗里刻花菱形开光装饰，开光内刻犀牛望月、莲荷纹等，是典型的金代纹饰。

元代耀州窑青釉产品质量进一步下降，胎粗厚，釉质泛黄者居多，纹饰粗糙。而多烧制具有磁州窑风格的白地黑花品种，一直延续到清代。

Yaozhou Kiln

The ceramic experts and scholars of the Palace Museum investigated the Yaozhou kiln in 1950s, 1970s, 1980s and 2006. The Yaozhou kiln founded in 1954 is located at Tongchuan City in Shaanxi Province. The specific site of Yaozhou kiln included Huangpuzhen, Chenlu, Lidipo, Shangdian, etc. As the largest area of heritage, the Huangpuzhen site was the most spectacular finding of investigation by the Palace Museum in 1950s.

The beginning of porcelain making in Yaozhou kiln can be dated back to the Tang dynasty, reached its prime time during the period of Northern Song dynasty, and ended in Yuan dynasty. Due to the large influence on kilns nearby, the system of kiln was formed with Yaozhou kiln at the center. In Tang dynasty, the Yaozhou kiln produced the ware of white glaze, black glaze, yellow glaze, black color on plain body, etc. The ware of black glaze was the largest in number, followed by white glaze, with celadon was the least. The tone of celadon could be divided into bluish yellow, grayish green and brownish yellow, both with thin glaze and dark grey body. The type of ware contained bowl, vase, pot, etc. The bowl with foot in shape of jade Bi was large in number, and the feature of having trace of 3 spur-marks at inner bottom was similar to kilns of Tang dynasty in Henan area. The ware of vase has the flat bottom mostly, and was covered with semiglaze. The condition mentioned above proved obviously the start-up phase of celadon ware in this period. Comparing with celadon, the black glaze ware was in high quality including the type of pot, vase, jar, basin, plate, box, etc. The black color painted on cover was a kind of unique variety. The design of black color painted on plain body has never seen before, so it could be said a new discovery. In Five Dynasties, the kiln made the ware in color of green, light green, bluish white, etc. The celadon ware has full glaze, and some ware with inscription of character "Guan" or with slender incised design. In recent years, a collection of wares in bluish white glaze including the type of bowl, bowl with floral-shaped mouth, saucer, vase in shape of double fish, Zun with lotus design, bowl with lotus design, and pot with incised design was excavated at kilns. Some experts regard the kiln as Chai kiln due to the delicate type, fine body, and glossy glaze of the wares mentioned above.

With the celadon as its main product, the Yaozhou kiln also produced a few brown glaze wares in Song dynasty. The carved design was the earliest appearance, and carved design and incised design were both used as stamped design started to produce after medium-term, and then stamped design became the main decorative method in later period. As one of the common decorative methods for ancient porcelain, the celadon with carved design used graver to engrave pattern on damp-dry body, then covered the glaze. As the most outstanding representative of ware with carved design in Song dynasty, the porcelain of Yaozhou kiln has the features of incisive cutting way, exquisite pattern and strong dimensionality. The celadon with stamped design was one of the familiar decorative methods for ancient porcelain. With the beginning at Western Jin, banding design and partial design was used in early period, and full stamped design in Song dynasty. The ware of plate and bowl with stamped design was in popular, and pottery mould was used in general. Expect of chrysanthemum design in common, the stamped design of Yaozhou kiln also included lotus, lotus leaf, children at play, seawater and fish, seawater and conch. In Jin dynasty, the stamped design used the layout method of carved the pattern into six equal parts.

The Yaozhou kiln was chosen by feudal official and began to produce porcelain with design of dragon and phoenix for the Court, which has obvious difference with folk porcelain. In 1953, a large number of plate and bowl remains with design of dragon and phoenix were excavated at outside of gate of pervasive peace (Guang'an Men) in Beijing, and the experts deduced that these wares were used for the Court by Yaozhou kiln. The plate remains with dragon design were also discovered in kiln of Yaozhou and this confirmed the deduction. As more evidence appeared, the wares also proved that the Yaozhou kiln presented the porcelain to the Court according to the book of *Record on Geographic Territory in Yuanfeng Period (Yuan Feng Jiu Yu Zhi)* by Wang Cun.

The porcelain sample with inscription of "Da An Er Nian" (the second year of Da'an period) and copper with inscription of "Zheng Long Tong Bao" (coin of Zhenglong period) were excavated at cultural layer of Jin dynasty in Huangpuzhen, and the excavated specimen has clear dissimilar with ware of Northern Song dynasty. The trace of a circle without glaze at inner bottom provided us with significant evidence of dating. The bowl with carved design such as rhinoceros looking at the moon, lotus and so on in diamond reserved panel was the typical pattern in Jin dynasty.

In Yuan dynasty, the product quality declined further including rough body, yellow glaze and coarse pattern, and the kiln was inclined to produce ware with black color on black ground, which was full of style of Cizhou kiln.

耀州窑遗址保护碑
The stele of kiln protection in Yaozhou kiln

耀州窑遗址出土窑具
The kiln furniture excavated at Yaozhou kiln

123　唐　白釉碗标本
Tang dynasty
Specimens of white glaze bowl

124　唐　白釉绿彩炉标本

Tang dynasty

Specimen of white glaze burner with green color

125　**唐　青釉碗标本**
Tang dynasty
Specimen of celadon bowl

126　**唐　黑釉双系瓶标本**
Tang dynasty
Specimens of black glaze pot with two handles

127　唐　黑釉执壶标本

Tang dynasty

Specimens of black glaze pot with handle

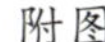

附图

唐　黑釉执壶

高 11.2 厘米　口径 4.8 厘米
足径 4.5 厘米
故宫博物院藏

Illustration
Tang dynasty
Black glaze pot with handle

Height 11.2cm, mouth diameter 4.8cm,
fooe diameter 4.5cm
Collection of the Palace Museum

壶撇口，长颈，溜肩，肩以下渐收至底，平底，实足。肩一侧置短流，另一侧饰曲柄。外壁施黑釉不到底。

此壶造型秀巧规整，胎质细腻，釉面温润，釉色漆黑纯正，是唐代耀州窑黑瓷产品中的佳作。

128　唐　黑釉器盖标本

Tang dynasty

Specimens of black glaze cover

129　**唐　黑釉盒盖标本**
Tang dynasty
Specimen of black glaze box cover

130　**唐　黑釉缸标本**
Tang dynasty
Specimen of black glaze vat

131　**唐　黑釉棺标本**
Tang dynasty
Specimen of black glaze coffin

132　唐　茶叶末釉执壶标本

Tang dynasty

Specimens of tea-dust glaze pot with handle

133　唐　茶叶末釉执壶标本

Tang dynasty

Specimen of tea-dust glaze pot with handle

附图

唐　茶叶末釉执壶

高 12 厘米　口径 4.2 厘米

足径 3.8 厘米

故宫博物院藏

Illustration

Tang dynasty

Tea-dust glaze pot with handle

Height 12cm, mouth diameter 4.2cm,
foot diameter 3.8cm

Collection of the Palace Museum

壶喇叭形撇口，长颈，溜肩，深腹，平底，实足。肩一侧置短流，另一侧置曲柄。外壁施茶叶末色釉不到底。

134　唐　素胎黑花罐标本

Tang dynasty

Specimen of unglazed jar with black color

附图

唐　素胎黑花钵

高 9.5 厘米　口径 11.1 厘米
足径 8.4 厘米
故宫博物院藏

Illustration
Tang dynasty
Unglazed earthen bowl in black color

Height 9.5cm, mouth diameter 11.1cm,
foot diameter 8.4cm
Collection of the Palace Museum

钵敛口，鼓腹，圈足。素胎，施化妆土。外壁饰间隔排列的黑褐色斑状纹及蔓草纹各三组。

素胎黑釉器是唐代耀州窑独创的一个品种，其制作工艺是先在成型的坯体上敷一层化妆土做底色，入窑素烧，其后再以黑釉彩料在素烧胎体上绘画花卉、蔓草纹饰，复入窑二次焙烧，烧成后黑釉彩料常凝结成釉凸起，与浅地色形成鲜明对比，极富装饰效果。

135　唐　素胎黑釉花卉纹盒盖标本
Tang dynasty
Specimen of unglazed box cover with floral design in black color

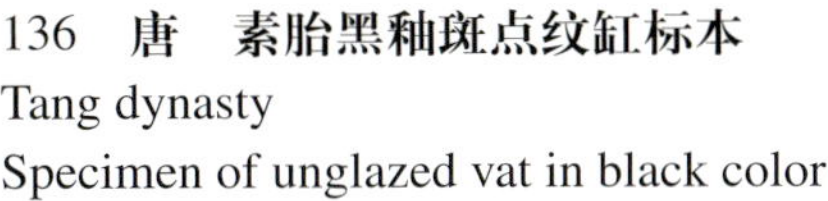

136　唐　素胎黑釉斑点纹缸标本
Tang dynasty
Specimen of unglazed vat in black color

137　唐　素胎黑釉花卉纹碗标本
Tang dynasty
Specimen of unglazed bowl with floral design in black color

138　五代　青釉碗标本

Five Dynasties

Specimens of celadon bowl

139 **五代 青釉碗标本**
Five Dynasties
Specimens of celadon bowl

140 **五代 青釉花式碗标本**
Five Dynasties
Specimens of celadon bowl in shape of petal

141 **五代 青釉盘标本**
Five Dynasties
Specimen of celadon plate

142 五代 青釉盘标本

Five Dynasties

Specimen of celadon plate

附图

五代 青釉葵瓣式盘

高 3.5 厘米 口径 13.5 厘米

足径 6.2 厘米

故宫博物院藏

Illustration

Five Dynasties

Petal-shaped celadon plate

Height 3.5cm, mouth diameter 13.5cm, foot diameter 6.2cm

Collection of the Palace Museum

盘五葵口，外壁压痕五道与之对应，浅弧腹，圈足宽矮，造型规整。通体施釉，釉色浅青，光亮莹润，口沿釉薄处呈酱黄色。足底为满釉支烧，边缘隐现细小支钉痕，是耀州窑五代时期常用的支烧方法。

陆游在《老学庵笔记》载："耀州出青瓷器，谓之越器，似以其类余姚县秘色也。"晚唐五代以来，越窑青瓷以其优秀的品质引来远近窑场的仿效，耀州窑、定窑等不少北方窑场也曾受到它的影响。此盘造型、釉色和装烧工艺即与越窑相似，不仅如此，五代至北宋早中期，耀州窑流行的线刻、浅浮雕式装饰，也带有追随越窑的痕迹。

143　五代　青釉划花碗标本
Five Dynasties
Specimens of celadon bowl

144 **宋 青釉瓶标本**
Song dynasty
Specimens of celadon vase

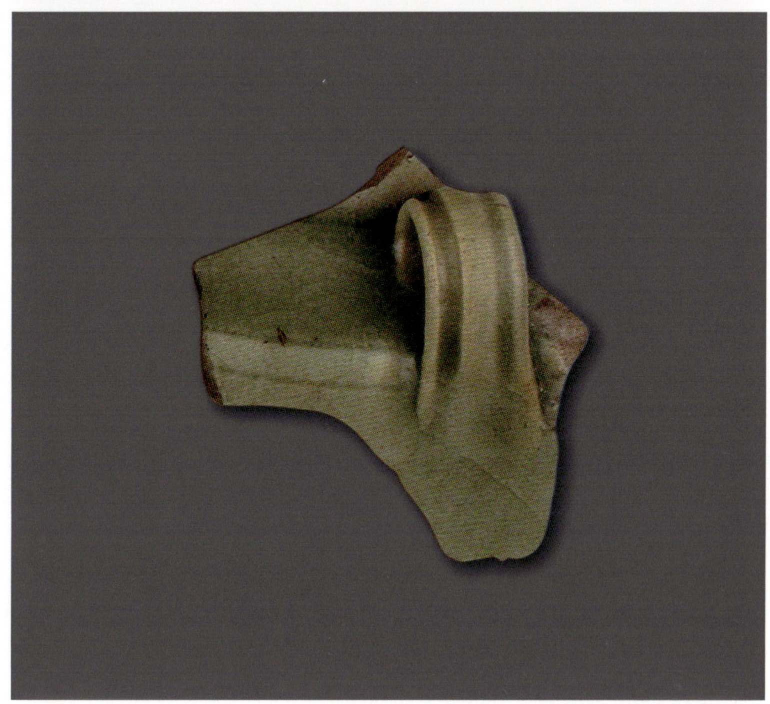

145 **宋 青釉双系罐标本**
Song dynasty
Specimen of celadon jar with two handles

146　宋　青釉壶标本
Song dynasty
Specimens of celadon pot

147　宋　青釉炉标本
Song dynasty
Specimens of celadon burner

148 **宋　青釉炉标本**

Song dynasty

Specimen of celadon burner

附图

宋　青釉炉

高 4.5 厘米　口径 5.9 厘米
足距 6.5 厘米
故宫博物院藏

Illustration
Song dynasty　Celadon burner

Height 4.5cm, mouth diameter 5.9cm, distance between feet 6.5cm
Collection of the Palace Museum

炉覆盘式宽沿，筒形腹底部内削，收成小平底，腹外壁贴五兽足。腹内及足底露胎，余处釉色青灰，有火烧的焦褐斑。

五足炉的造型较早见于唐代的熏炉，五代仍在使用。五足香炉主要流行在宋代，在耀州窑遗址北宋早期到南宋地层均有发现。此类炉有大小两种，造型相近，但大炉腹壁及宽沿多装饰华丽，五足兽面眉目清晰；小炉则多素面，相对简率。

149　**宋　青釉炉标本**

Song dynasty

Specimen of celadon burner

附图

宋　青釉炉

高5.2厘米　口径4.5厘米

足距5厘米

故宫博物院藏

Illustration

Song dynasty　Celadon burner

Height 5.2cm, mouth diameter 4.5cm, distance between feet 5cm

Collection of the Palace Museum

炉覆盘式宽沿，筒形腹底部内削，收成小平底，腹外壁贴五兽足。腹内及足底露胎，余处釉色青灰。

150 **宋 青釉盒标本**

Song dynasty

Specimens of celadon box

151 **宋 青釉碗标本**

Song dynasty

Specimen of celadon bowl

附图

宋　青釉碗

高 4.5 厘米　口径 11.3 厘米
足径 2.8 厘米
故宫博物院藏

Illustration
Song dynasty　Celadon bowl

Height 4.5cm, mouth diameter 11.3cm,
foot diameter 2.8cm
Collection of the Palace Museum

碗撇口，深弧腹，小圈足。通体施釉，釉色浅青，光亮莹润，口沿釉薄处呈酱黄色。底心釉面有火烧的焦褐斑，足底边缘刮釉露胎，粘连沙粒。

器物装烧时为避免粘连，多在窑床上铺垫沙层，高温下釉汁流淌，即发生粘沙现象，是烧造工艺上的缺陷之一。这类小碗除耀州窑外，河南临汝、宝丰、鲁山等瓷窑也有烧造。

152　宋　青釉碗标本

Song dynasty

Specimens of celadon bowl

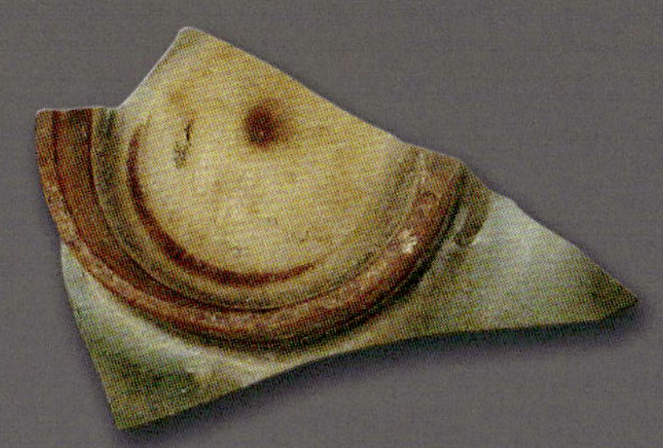

153　**宋　青釉碗标本**

Song dynasty

Specimen of celadon bowl

附图

宋　青釉花式碗

高 5 厘米　口径 11.3 厘米
足径 4 厘米
故宫博物院藏

Illustration
Song dynasty　Celadon bowl in shape of petal

Height 5cm, mouth diameter 11.3cm, foot diameter 4cm
Collection of the Palace Museum

碗呈五瓣花式状，口沿外撇，斜壁，圈足。内外壁自花式折沿处起棱线。通体施青釉，釉层较薄，釉面玻璃质感强并开细碎片纹。

这一时期耀州窑青瓷釉面皆玻璃质感强，施釉均匀，大多开有细碎片纹，釉面结合紧密没有剥釉现象。器物以日用瓷为主，在造型方面与五代耀瓷有明显的继承关系。

154　宋　青釉花式碗标本

Song dynasty

Specimen of celadon bowl in shape of petal

附图

北宋　青釉刻花花式碗

高 4.8 厘米　口径 17 厘米
足径 6 厘米
故宫博物院藏

Illustration
Northern Song dynasty
Celadon bowl with carved design in shape of petal

Height 4.8cm, mouth diameter 17cm, foot diameter 6cm
Collection of the Palace Museum

碗葵花式，腹部略有弧度，小圈足。通体施青釉。碗内刻满花卉纹，碗外划直线，线条纤细流畅。

花式碗，碗式之一，北宋以来较为常见，一般碗口沿至腹部为四瓣、六瓣、八瓣，宋代花式碗一般为六瓣。

155　**宋　青釉盘标本**

Song dynasty

Specimens of celadon plate

156　宋　青釉盘标本
Song dynasty
Specimen of celadon plate

157　宋　青釉刻花罐标本
Song dynasty
Specimens of celadon jar with carved design

158　宋　青釉刻花壶标本
Song dynasty
Specimen of celadon pot with carved design

159　**宋　青釉刻花花卉纹菊瓣盒标本**

Song dynasty

Specimen of celadon box with carved floral design in shape of chrysanthemum petal

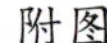

附图

宋 青釉刻花花卉纹菊瓣盒

高 5.9 厘米　口径 10.3 厘米
足径 7.3 厘米
故宫博物院藏

Illustration
Song dynasty
Celadon box with carved floral design in shape of chrysanthemun petal

Height 5.9cm, mouth diameter 10.3cm, foot diameter 7.3cm
Collection of the Palace Museum

盒扁圆，身浅腹折腰，圈足宽矮，盖侧壁窄直，顶面丰隆。器身与盖以子母口扣合，边缘呈细密菊瓣状。胎色浅灰，釉色浅青泛黄，底部无釉，显火石红色。盖面菊瓣纹内以斜刀广削法刻划五瓣花卉一株，叶片内篦划出筋脉。

河南的窑有与此盒相同的器物。

160 宋 青釉刻花器盖标本

Song dynasty

Specimens of celadon cover with carved design

161　宋　青釉刻花钱纹缸标本

Song dynasty

Specimen of celadon vat with carved copper design

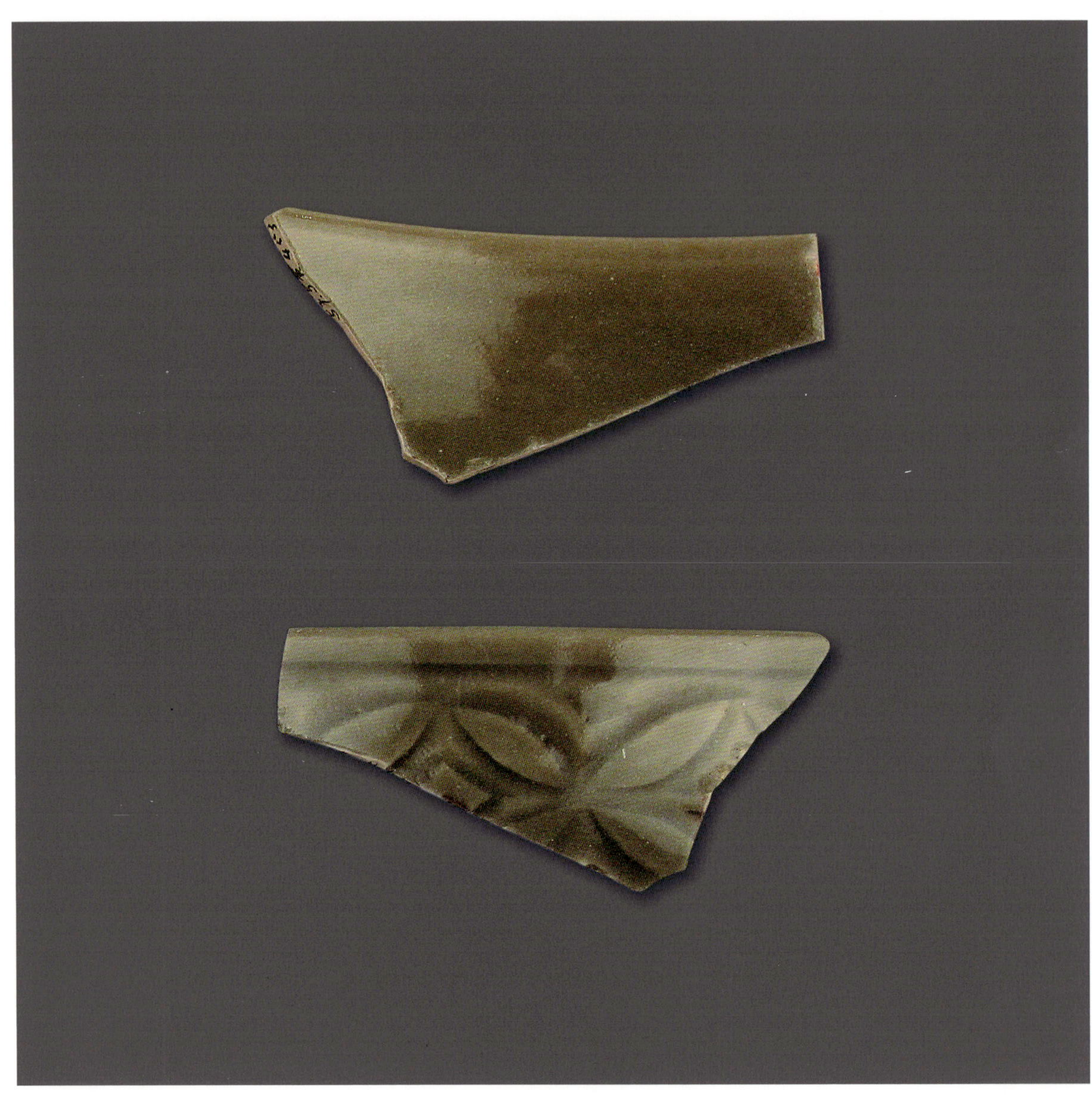

162　**宋　青釉刻花花卉纹碗标本**

Song dynasty

Specimens of celadon bowl with carved floral design

163　宋　青釉刻花花卉纹碗标本

Song dynasty

Specimens of celadon bowl with carved floral design

164 **宋　青釉刻花菊花纹碗标本**

Song dynasty

Specimens of celadon bowl with carved chrysanthemum design

165 **宋　青釉刻花水波纹碗标本**

Song dynasty

Specimen of celadon bowl with carved ripple design

166 宋 青釉刻花莲瓣纹碗标本

Song dynasty

Specimens of celadon bowl with carved lotus design

附图

北宋　青釉刻花莲瓣纹碗

高 7.5 厘米　口径 13 厘米
足径 4.5 厘米
故宫博物院藏

Illustration
Song dynasty　Celadon bowl with carved lotus design

Height 7.5cm, mouth diameter 13cm, foot diameter 4.5cm
Collection of the Palace Museum

碗口微撇，深腹，下内收，圈足。通体施青釉。外腹刻浮雕莲瓣纹，刀工犀利。

该碗为北宋早期制品。外腹莲瓣纹装饰是仿照浙江五代宋初的越窑青釉莲瓣纹碗特征制作的。

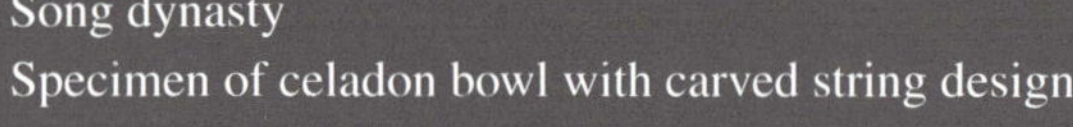

167　宋　青釉刻线纹碗标本

Song dynasty

Specimen of celadon bowl with carved string design

附图

宋　青釉里印花海水鱼纹外刻线纹碗

高 4.2 厘米　口径 10.7 厘米
足径 2.8 厘米
故宫博物院藏

Illustration
Song dynasty
Celadon bowl with stamped seawater and fish design inside and carved string design outside

Height 4.2cm, mouth diameter 10.7cm, foot diameter 2.8cm
Collection of the Palace Museum

碗撇口，斜壁，深腹，圈足。通体施青釉，釉色青中泛黄。碗心印花海水鱼纹，外壁饰凸线纹。

耀州窑瓷器上的刻花装饰于北宋中期发展成熟，到北宋末期工艺更为精细。此碗反映了耀州窑瓷器刻花工艺的突出成就，纹饰布局舒朗匀称，刻划技法娴熟传神，其所刻的直线纹在宋代青瓷上常可见到，是宋代流行的装饰纹样。

168　宋　青釉刻花鸭纹碗标本
Song dynasty
Specimen of celadon bowl with duck design

169
宋　青釉刻花婴戏纹碗标本
Song dynasty
Specimen of celadon bowl with carved design of children at play

170　**宋　青釉印花花卉纹“大观”铭文碗标本**

Song dynasty

Specimen of celadon bowl with stamped floral design and inscription of "Daguan"

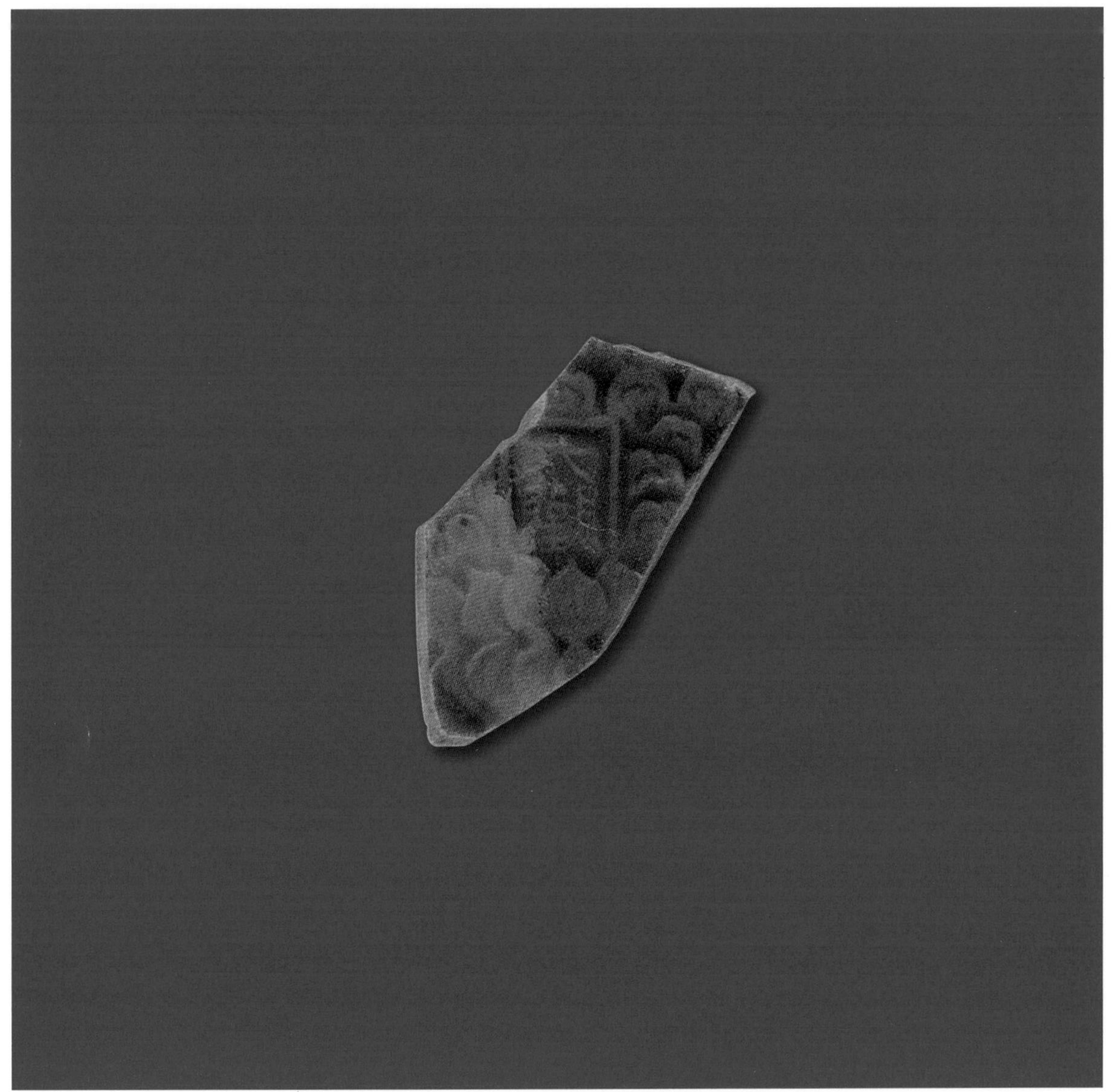

171　宋　青釉印花花卉纹碗标本

Song dynasty

Specimens of celadon bowl with stamped floral design

172　**宋　青釉里印花花卉纹外刻线纹碗标本**

Song dynasty

Specimens of celadon bowl with stamped floral design inside and carved string design outside

173　宋　青釉印花缠枝菊纹碗标本

Song dynasty

Specimens of celadon bowl with stamped entwined chrysanthemum design

174　**宋　青釉里印花缠枝菊纹外刻线纹碗标本**

Song dynasty

Specimen of celadon bowl with stamped entwined chrysanthemum design inside and carved string design outside

附图

宋 青釉里印花缠枝菊纹外刻线纹碗

高 9 厘米　口径 20 厘米
足径 5 厘米
故宫博物院藏

Illustration
Song dynasty
Celadon bowl with stamped entwined chrysanthemum design inside and carved string design outside

Height 9cm, mouth diameter 20cm,
foot diameter 5cm
Collection of the Palace Museum

碗撇口，斜壁，深腹，圈足。通体施青釉，釉色青中泛黄。碗心印缠枝菊纹，外壁饰凸线条纹。

耀州窑瓷器上的印花装饰于北宋中期出现，到北宋末期工艺更为精细。此碗反映了耀州窑瓷器印花工艺的突出成就，纹饰布局舒朗匀称，而又兼顾器形的特点，层层环绕，线条活泼流畅，具有耐人寻味的艺术效果。

175　**宋　青釉里印花水波纹外刻线纹碗标本**

Song dynasty

Specimen of celadon bowl with stamped ripple design inside and carved string design outside

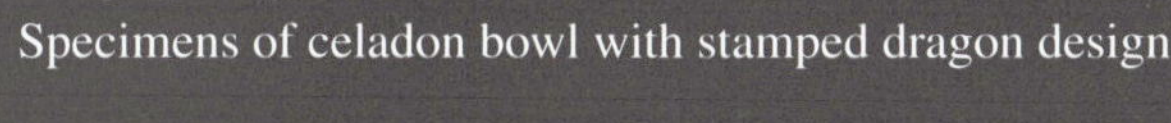

176　宋　青釉印花龙纹碗标本

Song dynasty

Specimens of celadon bowl with stamped dragon design

177　宋　青釉印花龙凤纹碗标本
Song dynasty
Specimens of celadon bowl with stamped dragon and phoenix design

178 宋 青釉印花龙凤纹碗标本

Song dynasty

Specimens of celadon bowl with stamped dragon and phoenix design

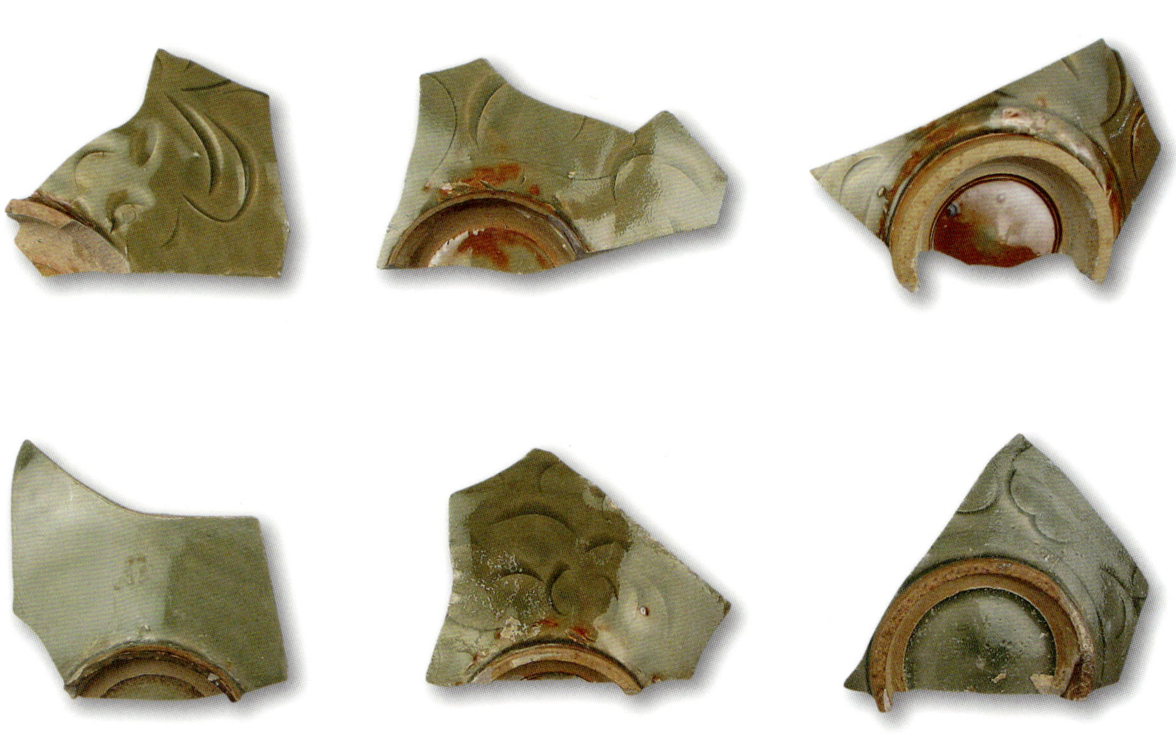

179 **宋　青釉印花龙凤纹碗标本**

Song dynasty

Specimens of celadon bowl with stamped dragon and phoenix design

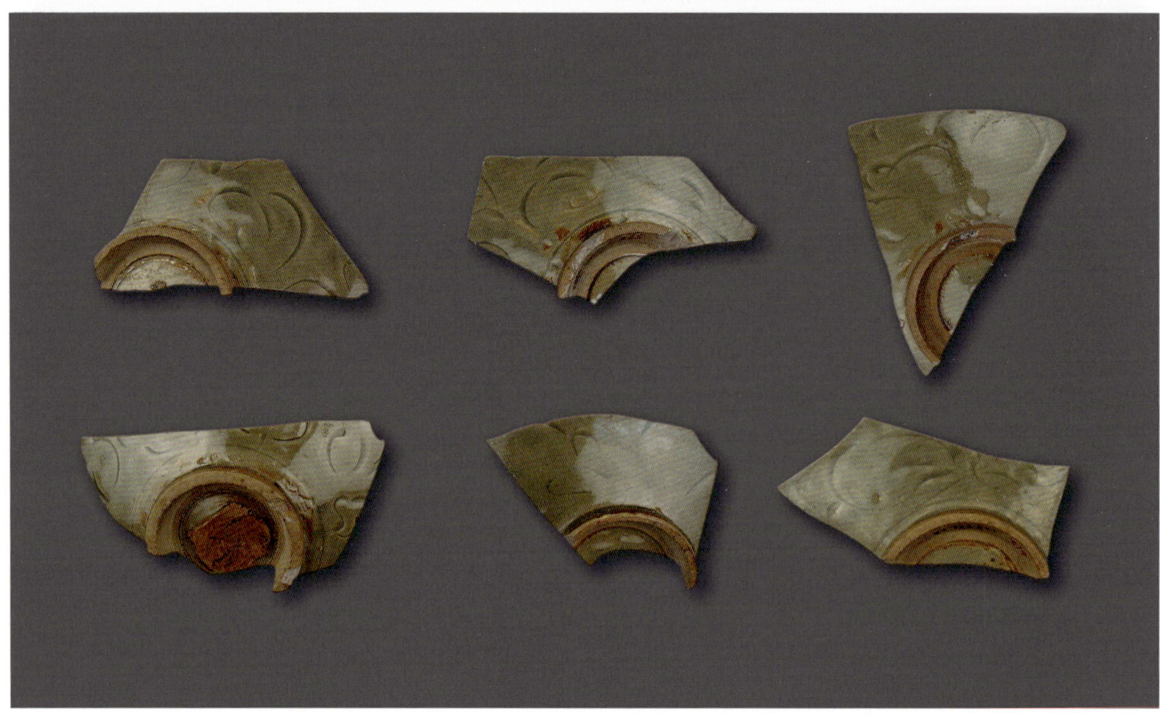

180 **宋 青釉印花龙凤纹碗标本**
Song dynasty
Specimen of celadon bowl with stamped dragon and phoenix design

181 **宋 青釉印花花卉纹盘标本**
Song dynasty
Specimens of celadon plate with stamped floral design

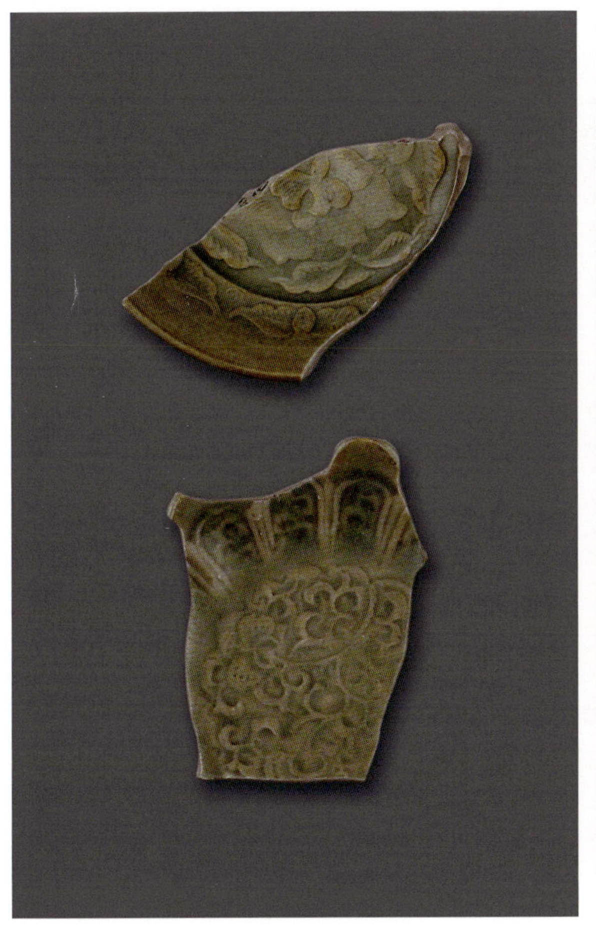

182　宋　青釉印花缠枝菊纹盘标本

Song dynasty

Specimens of celadon plate with stamped entwined chrysanthemum design

183　宋　青釉印花海水纹盘标本

Song dynasty

Specimen of celadon plate with stamped seawater design

184　**宋　黑釉壶标本**

Song dynasty

Specimen of black glaze pot

附图

元　黑釉双系罐

高 7 厘米　口径 5.5 厘米
足径 5.3 厘米
故宫博物院藏

Illustration

Yuan dynasty　Black glaze jar with two handles

Height 7cm, mouth diameter 5.5cm,
foot diameter 5.3cm
Collection of the Palace Museum

罐敛口，溜肩，肩部饰对称双环系，鼓腹，圈足。里满釉，外施黑釉不到底，釉色漆黑莹亮。

此罐造型规整，胎体厚重坚致，施釉匀净，釉色漆黑莹亮，是耀州窑宋、元时期黑釉瓷器的代表作。

185 宋 黑釉酱彩碗标本
Song dynasty
Specimen of black glaze bowl with dark reddish brown color

186 宋 酱釉瓶标本
Song dynasty
Specimen of dark reddish brown glaze vase

187 宋 酱釉碗标本
Song dynasty
Specimens of dark reddish brown glaze bowl

188　宋　酱釉碗标本

Song dynasty

Specimen of dark reddish brown glaze bowl

附图

宋　酱釉碗

高 4.5 厘米　口径 10.9 厘米
足径 3.1 厘米
故宫博物院藏

Illustration
Song dynasty
Dark reddish brown glaze bowl

Height 4.5cm, mouth diameter 10.9cm,
foot diameter 3.1cm
Collection of the Palace Museum

碗撇口，口唇稍厚，斜弧腹，小圈足。釉呈酱红色，匀净光亮，近足无釉，底露灰胎。

酱釉瓷是宋代耀州窑出现的新品种，有少量烧造。除耀州窑以外，河北的定窑、磁州窑，甘肃的安口窑，山西的介休窑，河南的修武窑、宝丰窑、鲁山窑等均有烧造。

189 宋 酱釉碗标本

Song dynasty

Specimen of dark reddish brown glaze bowl

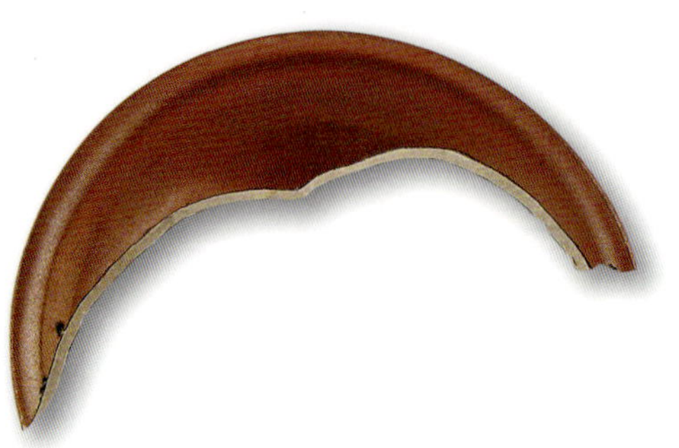

附图

宋 酱釉撇口碗

高 4.4 厘米 口径 14.6 厘米
足径 4.3 厘米
故宫博物院藏

Illustration
Song dynasty
Dark reddish brown glaze bowl

Height 4.4cm, mouth diameter 14.6cm, foot diameter 4.3cm
Collection of the Palace Museum

碗撇口，口唇稍厚，斜弧腹，小圈足。釉呈酱红色，匀净光亮，近足无釉，底露灰胎。

190 **宋　酱釉盘标本**

Song dynasty

Specimen of dark reddish brown glaze plate

191　金　青釉“大安二年”铭文罐标本

Jin dynasty

Specimen of celadon jar with inscription of "2nd of Da'an"

附图

宋（金）　青釉瓜棱小罐

高 4.7 厘米　口径 4.7 厘米

底径 4.5 厘米

故宫博物院藏

Illustration

Song dynasty (Jin dynasty)

Celadon melon-shaped jar

Height 4.7cm, mouth diameter 4.7cm,

bottom diameter 4.5cm

Collection of the Palace Museum

罐直口，短颈，丰肩，鼓腹，圈足。腹部压印瓜棱状凹痕 15 道，肩有弦纹数道。胎色浅灰，内施釉及唇，外施釉近底，釉色青绿，不均匀。

192 金 青釉刻花钱纹壶标本

Jin dynasty

Specimen of celadon pot with carved copper design

附图

金 青釉刻花钱纹小壶

高 13 厘米 口径 2.3 厘米
足径 6 厘米
故宫博物院藏

Illustration
Jin dynasty Celadon pot with carved copper design

Height 13cm, mouth diameter 2.3cm, foot diameter 6cm
Collection of the Palace Museum

壶圆口，垂腹，圈足，带盖，曲柄，湾流。通体施青黄色釉。口沿至器腹上部弦纹带内刻覆莲瓣纹，下部刻满钱纹。

钱纹是瓷器装饰的典型纹样之一，为圆圈中有内向弧形方格，似圆形方孔钱，多作二方或四方连续排列。在瓷器上始见于汉代，宋、元、明代较流行。

193 金 青釉刻花花卉纹盒标本

Jin dynasty

Specimens of celadon box with carved floral design

194 金 青釉刻花荷莲纹碗标本

Jin dynasty

Specimen of celadon bowl with carved lotus design

195　金　青釉刻花荷莲纹碗标本

Jin dynasty

Specimens of celadon bowl with carved lotus design

196 金 青釉刻花荷莲纹碗标本

Jin dynasty

Specimens of celadon bowl with carved lotus design

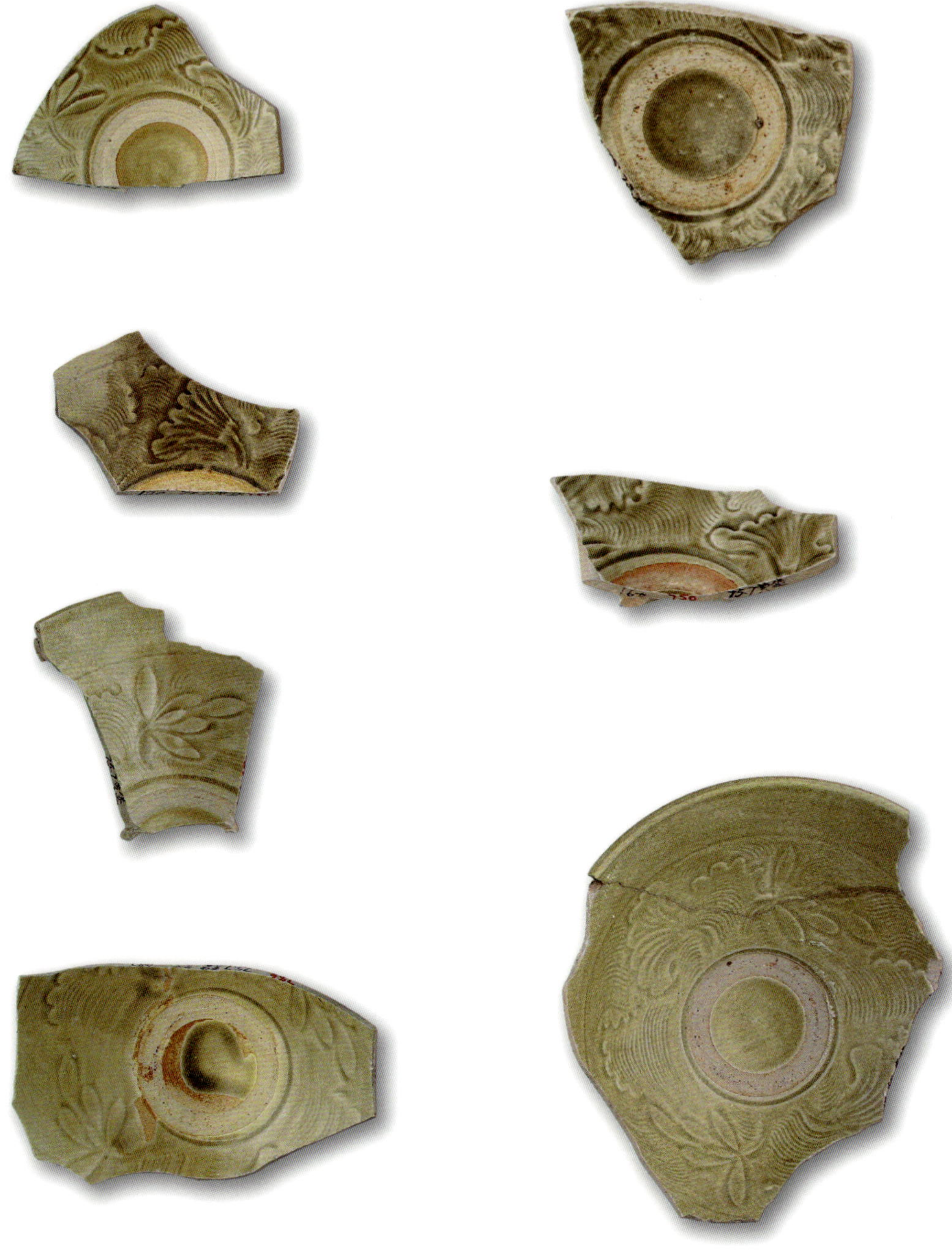

197　金　青釉刻花荷莲纹碗标本

Jin dynasty

Specimens of celadon bowl with carved lotus design

198　金　青釉刻花荷莲纹碗标本

Jin dynasty

Specimen of celadon bowl with carved lotus design

附图

金　青釉刻花荷莲纹碗

高 6.8 厘米　口径 18.8厘米

足径 5.8 厘米

故宫博物院藏

Illustration

Jin dynasty　Celadon bowl with carved lotus design

Height 6.8cm, mouth diameter 18.8cm, foot diameter 5.8cm

Collection of the Palace Museum

碗宽唇口，弧腹，圈足。通体施釉，釉色青中闪黄，足底边缘刮釉露胎，口沿釉薄处呈酱黄色。内壁刻一菱花形开光，中饰卷叶莲花一朵。

菱花形开光是金代耀州窑常见的开光形式，有开光花卉与开光犀牛纹。一花一叶纹除耀州窑外，磁州窑、定窑金代亦流行。

199　金　青釉刻花水波纹碗标本

Jin dynasty

Specimens of celadon bowl with carved ripple design

附图

金　青釉刻花水波纹碗

高 7.5 厘米　口径 19.5 厘米
足径 5.8 厘米
故宫博物院藏

Illustration
Jin dynasty　Celadon bowl with carved ripple design

Height 7.5cm, mouth diameter 19.5cm, foot diameter 5.8cm
Collection of the Palace Museum

碗唇口，弧腹，圈足。胎质粗糙，胎色黄褐，下腹及底无釉露胎，釉色青黄。内壁刻划水波纹六朵，外壁饰弦纹数道。足底满布铁锈色斑点，俗称“糊米底”，里心一圈刮釉，应采用涩圈叠烧法。

水波纹是陶瓷装饰的传统纹样，形象模拟流水的自然形态。专门描绘海水波涛的，通常叫“海水纹”或“海涛纹”；着意表现旋涡的，习惯称“旋涡纹”或“涡纹”。早在新石器时代，水波纹已经出现，马家窑文化彩陶上的水波纹，色彩单纯明快，线条优美流畅，是原始时代彩绘装饰的杰出代表。宋以来，水波纹大量运用在瓷器上，有的单独作为主题纹样，更多的是与其他纹样的组合，如宋代定窑、耀州窑的落花流水纹、海水游鱼纹等。

200 **金 青釉刻花水波纹碗标本**
Jin dynasty
Specimen of celadon bowl with carved ripple design

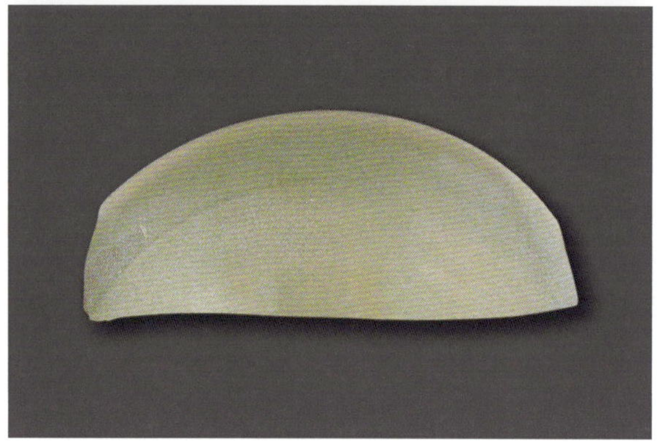

201 **金 青釉刻花犀牛纹碗标本**
Jin dynasty
Celadon bowl with carved rhinoceros design

附图

金　青釉刻花犀牛纹碗

高 7.3 厘米　口径 20.9 厘米
足径 6.1 厘米
故宫博物院藏

Illustration
Jin dynasty　Celadon bowl with carved rhinoceros design

Height 7.3cm, mouth diameter 20.9cm, foot diameter 6.1cm
Collection of the Palace Museum

碗宽唇口，弧腹，圈足。里外施青釉，底部无釉，呈灰黄色。内壁刻一菱花形开光，内刻一轮圆月高挂天空，下方一头水牛口部微张，前腿直立，后腿屈膝跪地，抬头仰望，菱形开光及水牛周边饰花卉纹。

此图案主要见于金代铜镜及定窑、耀州窑瓷器，传统认为是"犀牛望月"，后人考证提出应是"吴牛喘月"。据《世说新语》载："今之水牛唯生江淮间，故谓之吴牛也。南土多暑，而此牛畏热，见月疑是日，所以见月则喘。"

202　金　青釉刻花莲花纹八方盘标本

Jin dynasty

Specimen of celadon plate with carved lotus design

203　**金　青釉刻花水波纹盘标本**

Jin dynasty

Specimen of celadon plate with carved ripple design

204　金　青釉刻花水波纹盘标本

Jin dynasty

Specimen of celadon plate with carved ripple design

附图

金　青釉刻花水波纹洗

高 6.4 厘米　口径 12.2 厘米
足径 4 厘米
故宫博物院藏

Illustration
Jin dynasty
Celadon *Xi* with carved ripple design

Height 6.4cm, mouth diameter 12.2cm, foot diameter 4cm
Collection of the Palace Museum

洗敞口，浅壁，平底。内外施青釉，外底心素胎无釉。里心刻划水波纹。

耀州窑瓷器多为灰白胎，但多数器物透过青翠的釉层，使人感到的却是洁白、细腻的胎体，仿佛上釉前施一层化妆土。此洗即为一例。实际上这是由于胎土和釉料在加热烧成过程中产生化学反应，形成一层密合层所致。这种现象在河南临汝窑及钧窑产品中也可见到，这是由于它们的地质构成相近，坩土所含成分相似。

205　金　青釉模印狮形灯标本

Jin dynasty

Specimen of celadon light with stamped design in shape of lion

附图

金　青釉模印狮形灯

高 10.8 厘米　长 11.8 厘米
口径 9.9 厘米　足径 9.2×6 厘米
故宫博物院藏

Illustration
Jin dynasty　Celadon light with stamped design in shape of lion

Height 10.8cm, length 11.8cm,
mouth diameter 9.9cm,
foot diameter 9.2cm×6cm
Collection of the Palace Museum

灯呈狮形，继承唐代以来的雕塑形式，下有长方形底座。狮子站立，四肢肌肉发达，口微张，狮头、颈、尾模印卷曲的鬃毛，背有结带挂饰，背正中有柱，柱两面模印兽面纹。柱上承一托盘，托盘外口有弦纹一道，盘内刻荷花、荷叶纹。整体造型集实用与装饰于一体，狮子形象既温顺又生动。

从此器的釉色和纹饰看，具有典型的金代风格。耀州窑窑址金代地层出土有相似的器物。

206　金　青釉印花双鱼纹洗标本

Jin dynasty

Specimen of celadon *Xi* with stamped fish design

附图

金　青黄釉模印双鱼纹洗

高 3 厘米　口径 12 厘米
足径 5.3 厘米
故宫博物院藏

Illustration
Jin dynasty
Celadon *Xi* with stamped fish design

Height 3cm, mouth diameter 12cm,
foot diameter 5.3cm
Collection of the Palace Museum

洗圆口，折沿，圈足。通体施青黄色釉。内底模印双鱼纹。

鱼纹是陶瓷装饰的传统纹样之一。表现手法有刻划、彩绘、模印、贴塑等。最早见于新石器时代早期河姆渡文化陶器上，入宋以后，鱼纹题材广泛地被运用到瓷器上。

207 金 青釉印花花卉纹碗标本

Jin dynasty

Specimens of celadon bowl with stamped floral design

208　金　青釉印花荷莲纹盘标本
Jin dynasty　Specimen of celadon palte with stamped lotus design

209　金至元　白釉剔花刻字碗标本
From Jin to Yuan dynasty　Specimen of white glaze bowl with engraved design and characters

210　元　白地褐花花卉纹碗标本

Yuan dynasty

Specimens of white glaze bowl with floral design in brown color

211 元 里白釉点彩外黑釉碗标本

Yuan dynasty Specimen of bowl with white glaze and brown color inside and black glaze outside

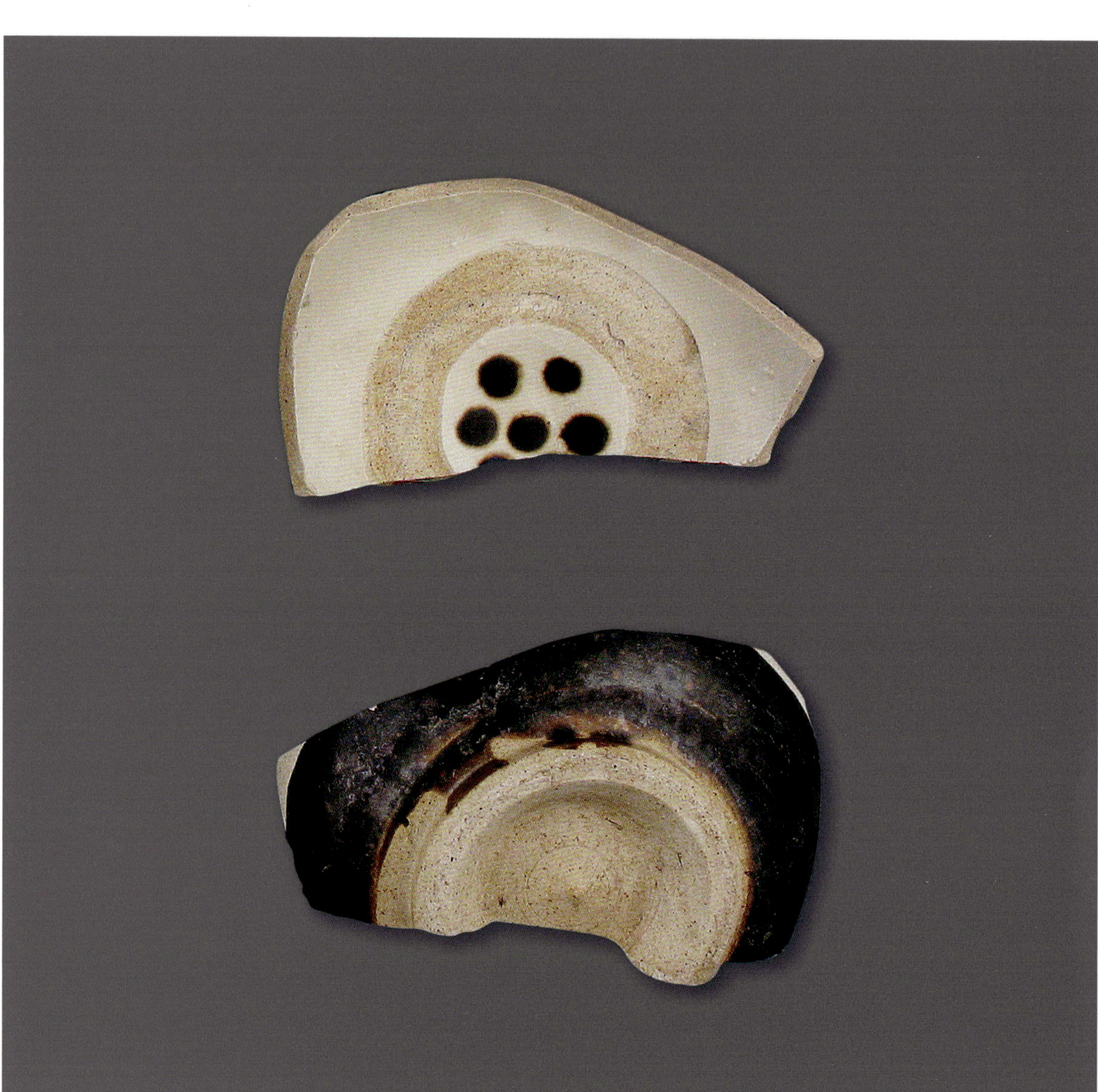

212　**宋至元　窑具标本**

From Song to Yuan dynasty

Specimens of kiln furniture

玉华宫遗址

遗址在陕西省西安市玉华宫。故宫博物院部分专家学者于20世纪70年代对该遗址进行了调查。遗址属宋代。主要有白釉瓷器，兼少量青釉、白地黑花瓷器。白釉器有碗、盘、盒等。器物胎体细白而坚致，釉质白而滋润，器物成型规矩，造型精巧，伴出有窑具。青釉器物中有的饰以划花装饰，与耀州窑同类器物相似。所采集的白釉标本质量较好，其窑口有待于进一步探讨。

The Heritage of Yuhuagong

The heritage is located at Yuhuagong in Xi'an, Shaanxi Province. The ceramic experts and scholars of the Palace Museum investigated the heritage in 1970s. With white glaze ware as its main product, the kiln which belongs to Song dynasty also produced ware in celadon and black color on white ground. The white ware contained bowl, plate, box, etc. The ware has the features of white and solid body, white and glossy glaze, well-behaved and delicate type. The kiln furniture was also excavated at the same time. The celadon ware also used the incised design, which was similar to the wares in Yaozhou kiln. The white glaze ware was in high quality, and the specific kiln was in need of further study.

213 **五代　青釉划花卷枝纹碗标本**

Five Dynasties

Specimens of celadon bowl with incised branch design

214　宋　白釉瓶标本
Song dynasty
Specimen of white glaze vase

215　宋　白釉罐标本
Song dynasty
Specimens of white glaze bowl

216　宋　白釉瓜棱罐标本
Song dynasty
Specimens of white glaze melon-shaped jar

217　宋　白釉炉标本
Song dynasty
Specimen of white glaze vat

218　**宋　白釉划花荷叶纹器盖标本**

Song dynasty

Specimens of white glaze cover with incised lotus leaf design

219 **宋　白釉碗标本**
Song dynasty
Specimen of white glaze bowl

220　宋　白釉碗标本

Song dynasty

Specimens of white glaze bowl

221 宋 白釉碗标本

Song dynasty

Specimens of white glaze bowl

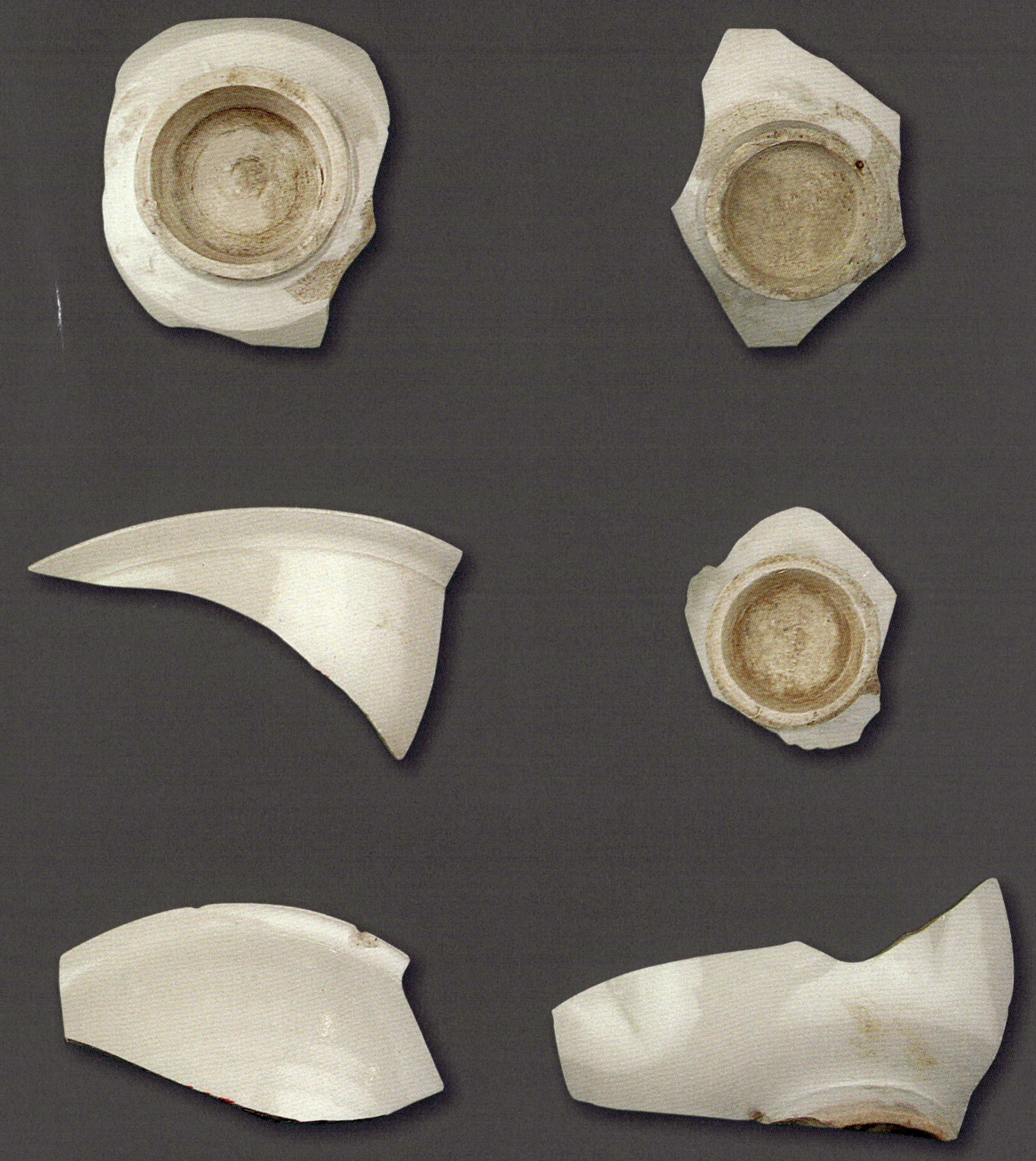

222　宋　白釉盘标本

Song dynasty

Specimens of white glaze plate

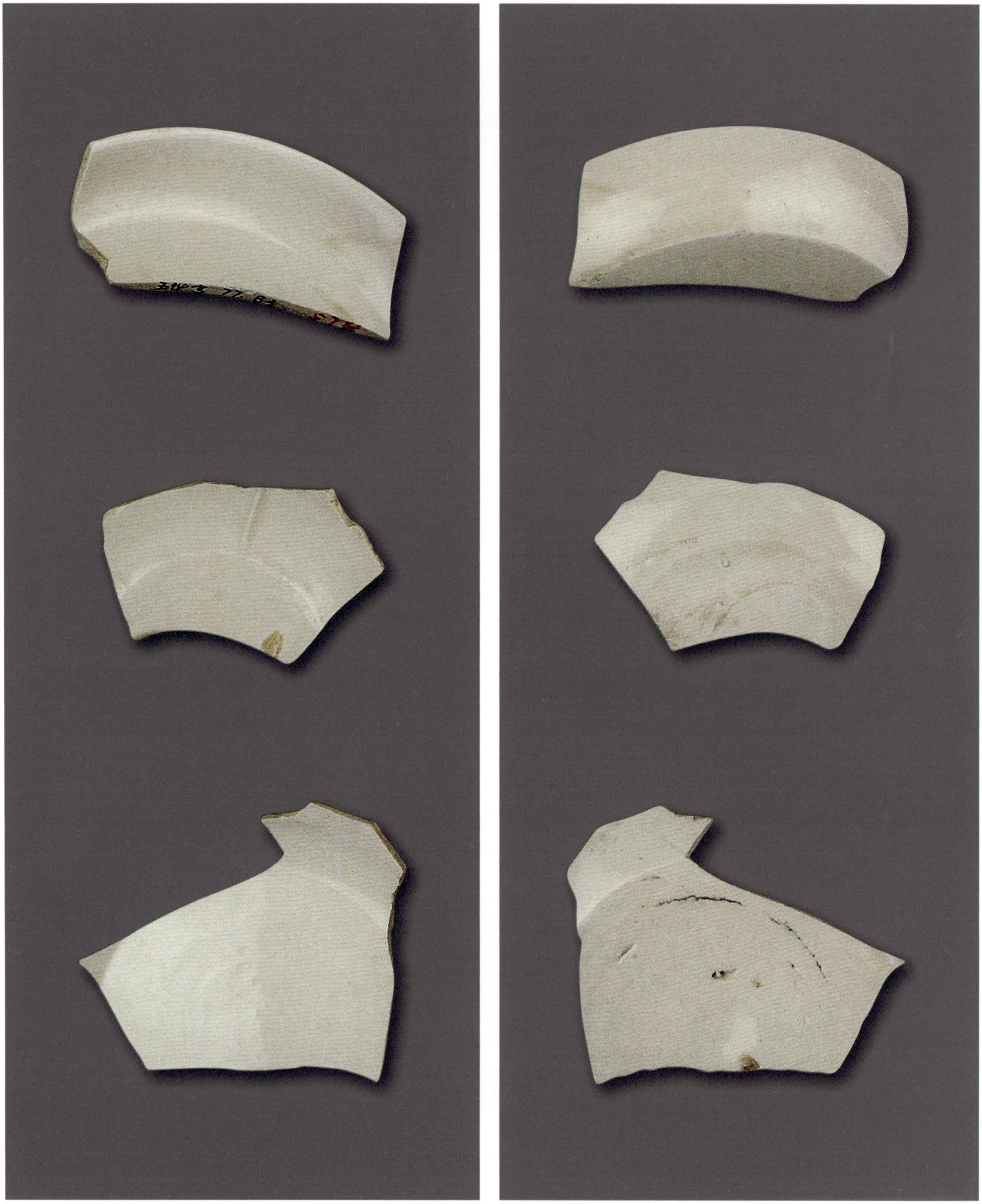

223 宋 白釉雕塑标本
Song dynasty
Specimen of white glaze figure

224 宋 白釉划花荷叶纹器盖标本
Song dynasty
Specimen of white glaze cover with incised lotus leaf design

225 宋 青釉炉标本
Song dynasty
Specimen of celadon burner

226 **宋　青釉碗标本**

Song dynasty

Specimens of celadon bowl

227　宋　青釉花式碗标本
Song dynasty
Specimen of celadon bowl in shape of petal

228　宋　青釉刻线纹碗标本
Song dynasty
Specimen of celadon bowl with carved string design

229 宋 青釉印花花卉纹碗标本

Song dynasty

Specimens of celadon bowl with stamped floral design

旬邑窑

故宫博物院部分专家学者于 20 世纪 60 年代、70 年代以及 2006 年对该窑进行了调查。旬邑窑在陕西省耀州窑西南 70 公里的旬邑县安仁，主要为金代瓷窑。以烧青釉为主，兼烧黑釉、酱釉器物。青釉釉色偏黄者较多，有刻花、印花装饰，碗心多一圈无釉，与金耀州窑具有同样风格。纹饰有刻花、篦划水波纹及荷叶纹等，亦与耀州窑布局方法基本相同。2006 年调查该窑时，正值修公路，窑址标本散落于地表，采集的标本有的釉色很好，与耀州窑色好者近似，难分伯仲。从而改变了旬邑窑瓷器质量较差、釉色不好的传统认识。该窑基本属耀州窑系范畴。

Xunyi Kiln

The ceramic experts and scholars of the Palace Museum investigated the Xunyi kiln in 1960s, 1970s and 2006. The kiln site is located at Xunyi County in Shaanxi Province, which is 70km far from Yaozhou kiln in southwest. With celadon as its main product, the kiln which belongs to Jin dynasty also produced ware in black glaze and brown glaze. The celadon ware with yellow gloss was large in number, and the decoration method included incised design and stamped design. A circle without glaze at inner bottom of bowl was similar to Yaozhou kiln of Jin dynasty. The design of carved ripple design and lotus design was also as same as layout of ware in Yaozhou kiln. Due to the highway work, the specimens were scattered at surface in investigation of 2006. The collected specimen in high quality was equally prosperous to Yaozhou kiln. The fact changed the understanding of poor quality and wrong glaze about ware in Xunyi kiln. The Xunyi kiln belongs to the system of Yaozhou kiln.

旬邑（安仁）窑遗址保护碑
The stele of kiln protection in Xunyi (Anren) kiln

旬邑窑遗址
The heritage of Xunyi kiln

230　金　青釉印花花卉纹碗标本

Jin dynasty

Specimens of celadon bowl with stamped floral design

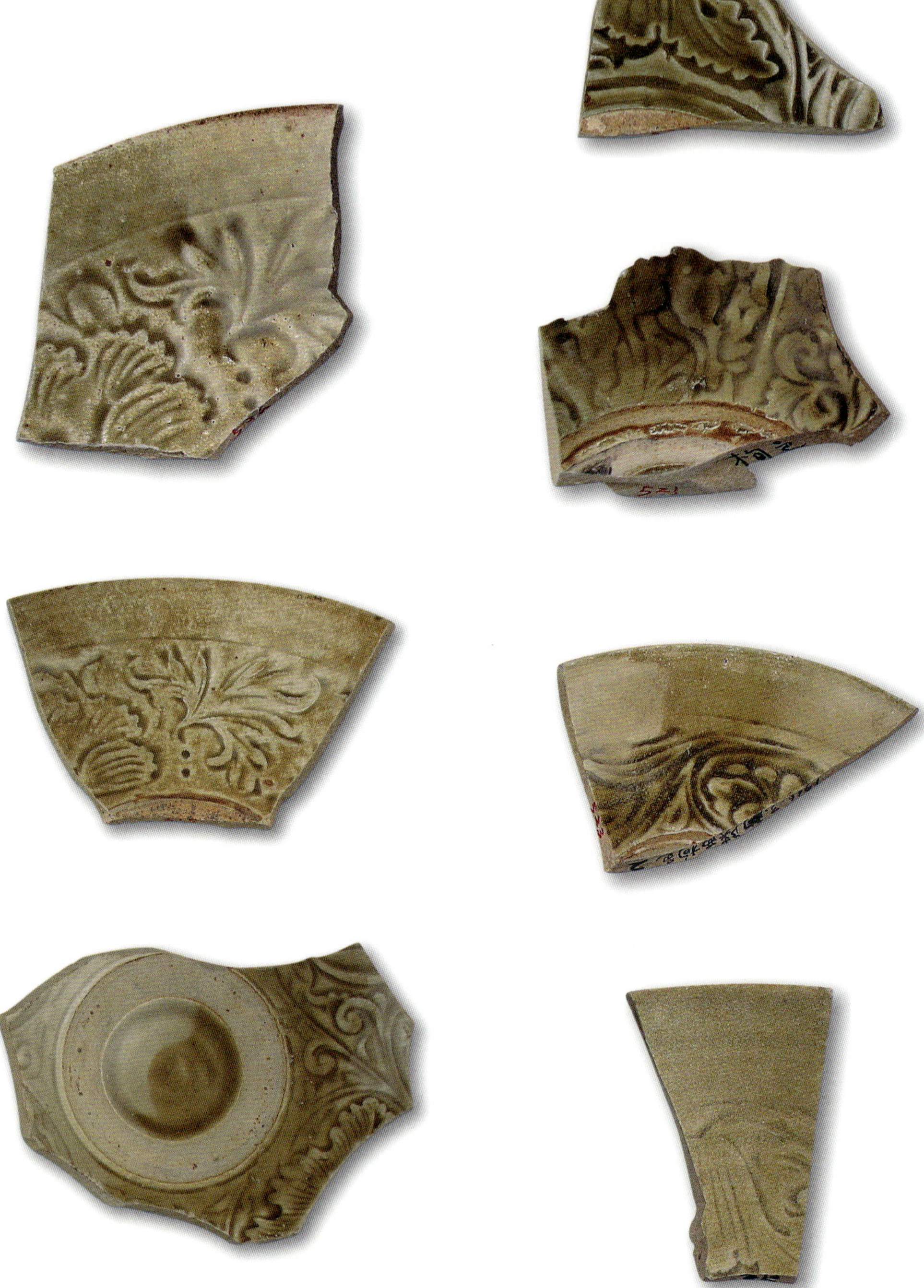

231　**金　青釉印花水波纹碗标本**

Jin dynasty

Specimens of celadon bowl with stamped ripple design

232　金　青釉刻花菱形开光卷枝纹碗标本
Jin dynasty
Specimen of celadon bowl with carved branch design in reserved panel

233　金　黑釉瓶标本
Jin dynasty
Specimens of black glaze vase

234　金　黑釉罐标本
Jin dynasty
Specimens of black glaze jar

235　金　黑釉壶标本
Jin dynasty
Specimens of black glaze pot

236　**金　酱釉壶标本**
Jin dynasty
Specimen of dark reddish brown glaze pot

237　**金　酱釉灯标本**
Jin dynasty
Specimen of dark reddish brown glaze light

238　**金　酱釉器盖标本**
Jin dynasty
Specimen of dark reddish brown glaze cover

239 **金 酱釉碗标本**

Jin dynasty

Specimen of dark reddish brwon glaze bowl

240　**金　酱釉点彩碗标本**

Jin dynasty

Specimens of dark reddish brwon glaze bowl with color spots

澄城窑

2006年故宫博物院的部分专家学者对该窑进行了调查。据明代文献记载澄城窑唐代已开始烧瓷器，窑火不断直至现代。有可靠实物资料证实该窑从明万历时期烧造瓷器，晚清民国兴盛，保存至今的窑炉中有“道光年”（1821～1850年）、“咸丰元年”（1851年）铭文砖。其中保存较好的窑炉，至今仍可使用。目前澄城尧头窑东山与西山两大片相连的古窑遗址群，仍存30座古窑，方圆五平方公里，匣钵、瓷片堆积丰富，与以窑神庙为中心的百余家窑工民居的窑头古镇构成了规模宏伟的古窑陶瓷文化遗存，这在国内外是比较罕见的。

从实物及标本来看，澄城窑在烧瓷品种、装饰风格、器物造型等方面都与北方河北、山西、陕西、甘肃、宁夏等地区瓷窑的产品有不同程度的相似。在其发展兴盛时期，主要烧制黑釉瓷器，装饰主要有剔花、印花、划花、贴花、雕塑等。其中的老鼠罐是该窑最具特色的作品。除黑釉外，还烧造酱釉、褐釉、茶叶末釉、青釉、青釉刻花、白釉、白釉印花、白釉刻花、白釉剔花、白地黑花、青花等品种。装饰题材丰富，有花卉、动物、人物等。在各类器物上书写文字也是该窑的一大特色，有书写“福”、“寿”、“天下太平”、“天地会”、“忠信孝弟”、“高枕而眠”、“玉堂佳器”、“状元红”、“三元酒”、“管好小娃”及诗句等，还有纪年款，如“康熙二十四年”、“乙亥”（康熙三十四年）、“雍正元年”、“咸丰二年”、“咸丰十一年”、“道光五年”、“民国十八年”、“民国二十一年”、“民国二十四年”直至“1950年”铭文的瓷器或窑具，为器物断代提供了可靠的依据。从总体来看，该窑是一处具有浓郁地方特色的瓷窑。

Chengcheng Kiln

The ceramic experts and scholars of the Palace Museum investigated the Chengcheng kiln in 2006. According to the archives of Ming dynasty, the Chengcheng kiln started porcelain making at Tang dynasty, and had a continuous firing till now. The reliable documents confirmed that kiln produced porcelain from Wanli reign of Ming dynasty and thrived in late Qing dynasty and a period of the Republic of China. The inscription brick with “Daoguang Reign” and “1st year of Xianfeng” was still kept in kiln furnace. The kiln furnace in well condition still worked at present. The kiln site, which covers 5km, linked the two heritages including Dongshan and Xishan, and has various remains containing sagger, porcelain chips and 30 kilns. The ancient kiln remains which centered in Temple of Kiln God and contained dwellings for kiln workers and ancient towns were rare in domestic and abroad.

Based on cultural relics and specimens, it was confirmed that the ware of Chengcheng kiln that was in Hebei, Shanxi, Shaanxi, Gansu, Ningxia and so on contained the aspect of variety, decoration style, type, etc. With black glaze ware as its main product in palmy days, the decoration method of the kiln included engraved design, stamped design, incised design, appliqué design, sculpture, etc. The mouse jar was the characteristic ware in Chengcheng kiln. Besides, the kiln also made ware of dark brown glaze, brown glaze, tea dust glaze, celadon, celadon with engraved design, white glaze, white glaze with stamped design, white glaze with cut design, white glaze with engraved design, black color on white ground, blue-and-white, etc. The decorative theme contained floral, animal, figure, etc. The ware with characters was also the typical one, including “Fu”, “Shou”, “Tian Xia Tai Ping”, and “Tian Di Hui”, “Zhong Xin Xiao Di”, “Gao Zhen Er Mian”, “Yu Tang Jia Qi”, “Zhuang Yuan Hong”, “San Yuan Jiu”, “Guan Hao Xiao Wa”, poems, etc. The dating mark was also used in ware and kiln furniture, contained “24th of Kangxi Reign”, “Yi Hai” (43th of Kangxi Reign), “1st of Yongzhen Reign”, “2nd of Xianfeng Reign”, “11th of Xianfeng Reign”, “5th of Daoguang Reign”, “18th of the Republic of China”, “21st of the Republic of China”, “24th of the Republic of China”, “the year of 1950”, and provided us with reliable basis of dating. In general, the Chengcheng kiln was the one that was full of local flavor.

澄城窑窑炉遗址
The kiln heritage of Chengcheng kiln

澄城窑遗址瓷片堆积
The porcelain shred accumulation of Chengcheng kiln

241　**明　青釉碗标本**
Ming dynasty
Specimen of celadon bowl

242　**明　青釉剔花梅花纹碗标本**
Ming dynasty
Specimen of celadon bowl with engraved plum blossom design

附图

明　青釉剔花八宝纹双耳罐

高 17.5 厘米　口径 15 厘米
底径 13 厘米
2007 年尧头镇浴子河村出土

Illustration
Ming dynasty　Celadon jar with two ears and engraved design of the Eight Treasures

Height 17.5cm, mouth diameter 15cm, bottom diameter 13cm
Excavated at Yuzihe Village, Yaotou County in 2007

罐直口，短颈，长弧腹，平底。通体施青釉，釉面莹亮透明，釉色为淡豆青色，腹部釉下剔刻八宝纹。

澄城窑青釉瓷，以晚明至清初的产品最为精致，釉面薄而透明，釉色豆青，釉下多有剔刻花纹饰，别具一格。这种独特的青釉釉下剔刻花装饰技法的制作方法是在色调较深的胎体上先敷一层精细洁白的化妆土，然后在化妆土上以刀具剔刻出花纹再罩透明青釉入窑烧成，在透亮釉面映衬下的纹样清晰而明丽。

243　**明　青釉褐彩印字碗标本**

Ming dynasty

Specimens of celadon bowl with stamped character in brown color

附图

明　酱釉印"福"字盘

高 3.5 厘米　口径 20 厘米
足径 8.6 厘米

Illustration
Ming dynasty
Dark reddish brown glaze plate with stamped character "Fu"

Height 3.5cm, mouth diameter 20cm, foot diameter 8.6cm

盘敞口，弧壁，圈足。里外施酱釉，釉面莹润，盘心无釉，并模印一阳文"福"字，外环一周宽阔的刮釉露胎痕及垫圈留下的粗糙沙粒，这反映出明代尧头窑烧造碗、盘类民用瓷多采用这种低成本的垫圈叠烧方法来提高产量。

244 明 酱釉碗标本

Ming dynasty

Specimens of dark reddish brown glaze bowl

245　明至清　白釉碗标本
From Ming to Qing dynasty
Specimens of white glaze bowl

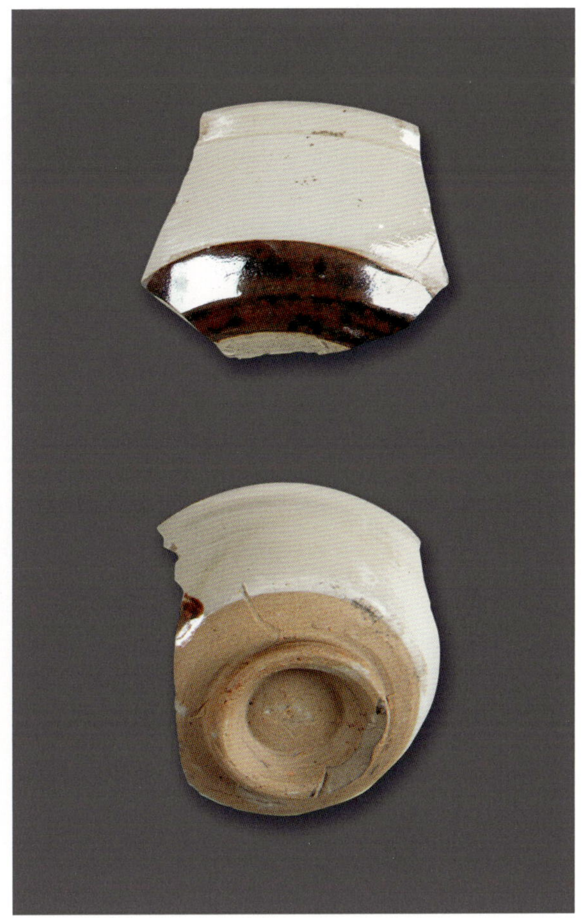

246
明至清　白地褐花花卉纹碗标本
From Ming to Qing dynasty
Specimen of white glaze bowl with floral design in brown color

247 明至清 白地褐花花卉纹碗标本

From Ming to Qing dynasty

Specimens of white glaze bowl with floral design in brown color

248 **明至清　白地褐花菊花纹碗标本**

From Ming to Qing dynasty

Specimen of white glaze bowl with chrysanthemum design in brown color

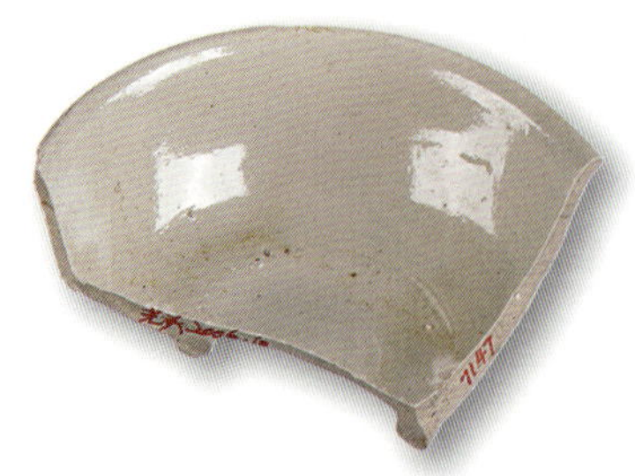

附图

清晚期 白地褐花菊花纹碗

高 6 厘米　口径 9 厘米
足径 4 厘米

Illustration
Late Qing dynasty　White glaze bowl with chrysanthemum design in brown color

Height 6cm, mouth diameter 9cm, foot diameter 4cm

碗唇口微撇，深弧腹，圈足。通体施白釉，足墙无釉露胎。外壁饰褐彩折枝菊花纹。

澄城窑白地褐彩瓷器装饰纹样题材丰富，常见各式花卉如梅花、菊花、莲花及蝴蝶、神鸟、婴戏、八卦、鱼网纹等，纹饰绘画笔法简练流畅，形象描绘夸张，具有民间美术质朴洒脱的艺术风格，此碗可称代表。

249 **明至清　白釉绞化妆土碗标本**
From Ming to Qing dynasty
Specimen of twisted glaze bowl

250 **明至清　里白釉外酱釉碗标本**
From Ming to Qing dynasty
Specimen of bowl with white glaze inside and dark reddish brown glaze outside

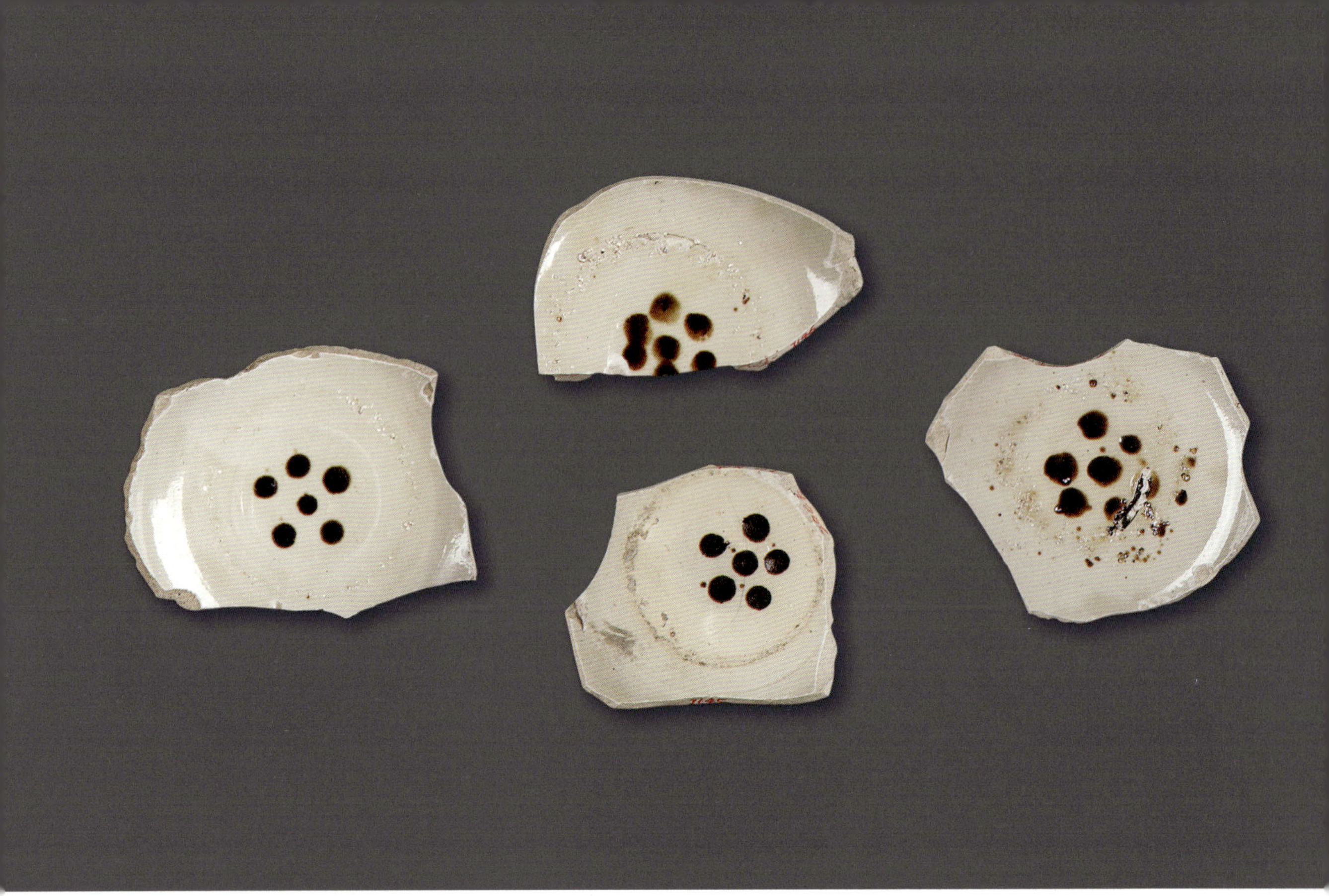

251 明至清 里白釉点彩外酱釉碗标本

From Ming to Qing dynasty
Specimens of white glaze bowl with brown color design inside and dark reddish brown glaze outside

附图

明至清 白釉点彩碗

高 3.3 厘米 口径 20 厘米
足径 8.5 厘米

Illustration
From Ming to Qing dynasty White glaze bowl with brown color design

Height 3.3cm, mouth diameter 20cm, foot diameter 8.5cm

碗敞口，弧壁，圈足。通体施白釉，里壁和盘心施褐色点彩四组，外围褐彩弦纹边饰。

白地褐彩又称“白地铁绣花”，是澄城窑瓷器代表性的装饰技法之一，明清时期均有生产。其产品特点是在略显粗糙的黄色胎体上施化妆土，然后以含氧化铁的材料绘画花纹，再罩透明釉烧成。而点状梅花纹为尧头窑白地褐彩器中常见的纹饰题材，除此盘所绘七点梅花外，尚有五点、六点、八点、九点的梅花纹。

252　明至清　里白釉点彩外酱釉碗标本

From Ming to Qing dynasty

Specimens of white glaze bowl with brown color design inside and dark reddish brown glaze outside

253 **明至清　黑釉双系瓶标本**
From Ming to Qing dynasty
Specimen of black glaze jar with two handles

附图

明　黑釉双系瓶

高 29 厘米　口径 12.5 厘米
足径 23 厘米
澄城窑博物馆藏

Illustration
Ming dynasty
Black glaze vase with two handles

Height 29cm, mouth diameter 12.5cm, foot diameter 23cm
Collection of the Chengcheng Kiln Museum

瓶碗形口，短束颈，溜肩，鼓腹，圈足微外撇，颈肩处饰双系。通体施黑釉，外施釉不到底，釉色漆黑光亮。

明代澄城窑烧造出许多器形较大的黑釉瓶、壶、坛类器皿。质朴的造型，漆黑的釉色，体现出这些民用瓷器特有的韵味。

254　明至清　黑釉瓶标本
From Ming to Qing dynasty
Specimen of black glaze vase

255　明至清　黑釉罐标本
From Ming to Qing dynasty
Specimens of black glaze jar

256 **明至清　酱釉罐标本**
From Ming to Qing dynasty
Specimen of dark reddish brown glaze jar

257 **明至清　酱釉灯标本**

From Ming to Qing dynasty

Specimens of dark reddish brwon glaze light

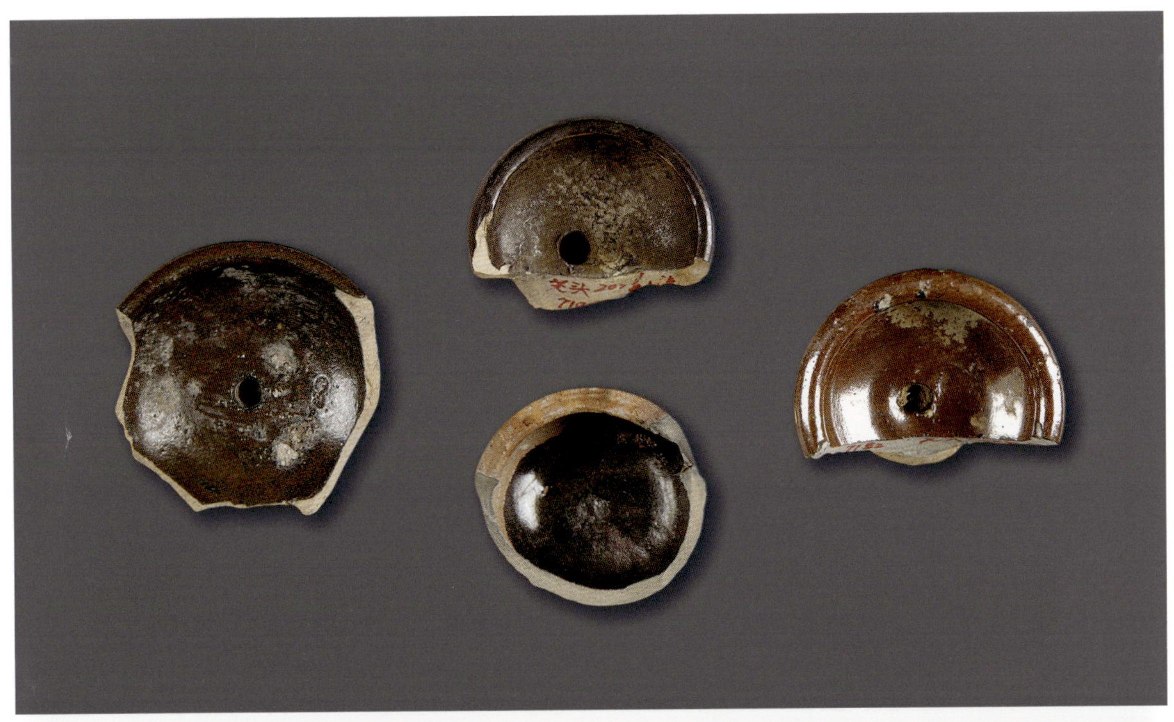

258　**清　黑釉老鼠罐标本**

Qing dynasty

Specimen of black glaze jar with knob in shape of rat

附图

清晚期　黑釉老鼠罐（一组）

Illustration

Late Qing dynasty　Set of covered jar with knob in shaped of rat

罐子母口，深腹，平底，盖拱形，盖顶饰鼠钮。通体施黑釉，釉色漆黑莹亮。

黑釉瓷器是澄城窑自创烧以来就盛烧不衰的主流产品，在大量生产的碗、盘、炉、罐、瓶、壶、坛等民用瓷中，老鼠罐或称鼠钮罐是最具特殊风格的一种黑瓷造型。其特征为在罐盖顶部塑一脊背高隆，尖嘴，圆耳，拖着长尾似在爬行的老鼠作为盖的提钮。鼠（子鼠）为十二生肖之首，生命力顽强旺盛，在当地民俗文化中也有以鼠为“繁衍之神”的子神之意，自清代出现后，直到今天都是澄城窑生产的一种具有独特造型的黑瓷品种。

259　明至清　窑具标本
From Ming to Qing dynasty
Specimens of kiln furniture

宁夏

2005年、2006年故宫博物院的部分专家学者对该地区的瓷窑进行了调查。宁夏地区瓷窑主要在灵武，有回民巷窑及磁窑堡窑等。近些年发现的下河沿窑还有待于调查。该地区烧制的瓷器在品种、装饰方法、制作工艺等方面与北方很多瓷窑，特别是磁州窑有相似之处，但在造型和装饰上有自身的特点。

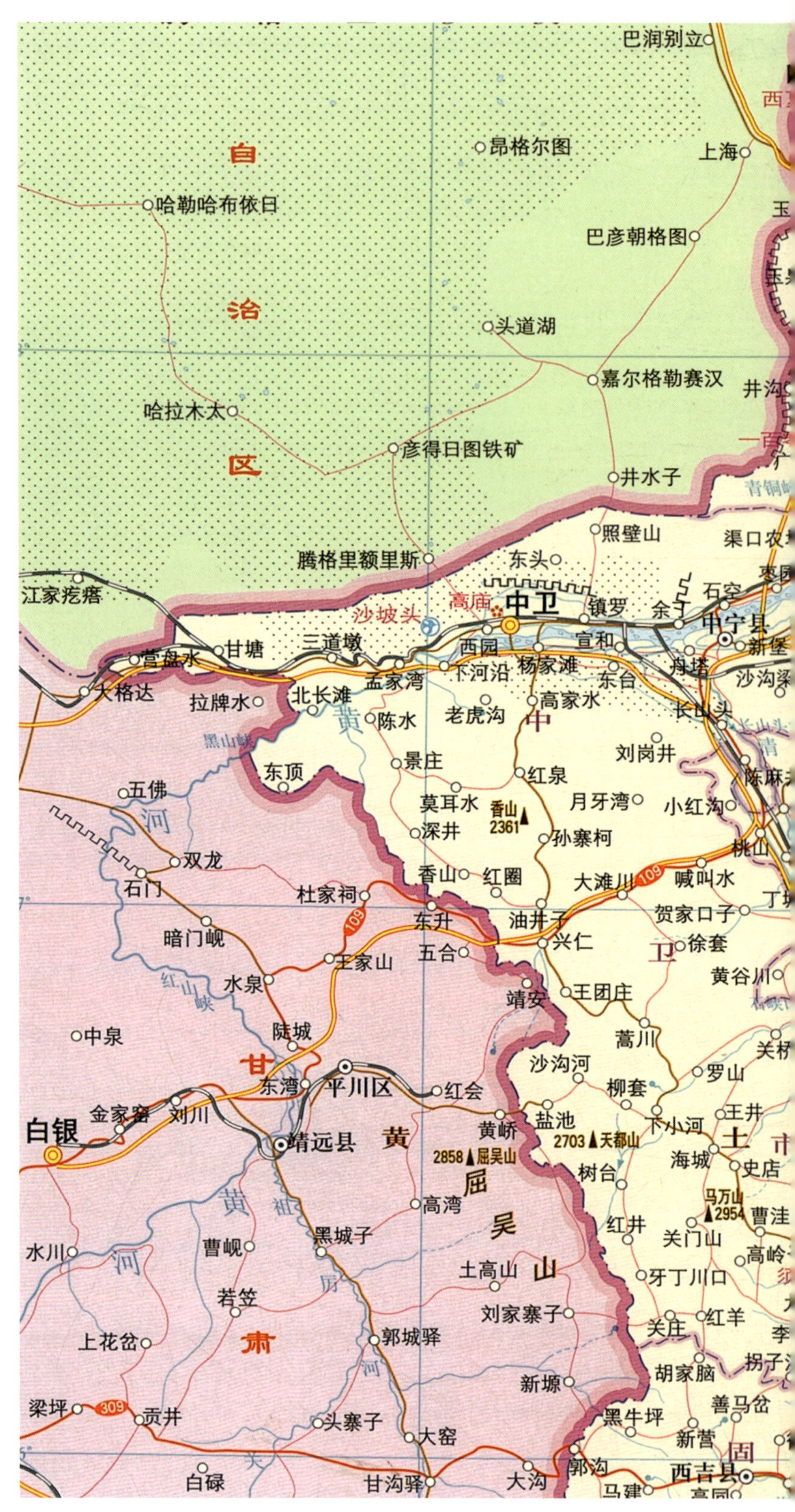

宁夏窑址分布图

Ningxia Hui Autonomous Region

The ceramic experts and scholars of the Palace Museum investigated the kilns of Ningxia in 2006. The main kilns of Ningxia Region most located in Lingwu, such as Huiminxiang kiln, Cibao kiln, etc. The Xiaheyan kiln founded in recent years still needs a further investigation. Although the porcelain variety, decorative method and firing technology of kilns were similar to kilns in northern part of China, especially with the Cizhou kiln, the kilns still has its own feature in type and decoration.

The Distribution Map of Kilns in Ningxia Hui Autonomous Region

灵武窑

灵武窑主要包括磁窑堡窑和回民巷窑两处窑址。

磁窑堡窑，窑址在灵武市东约 35 公里的煤矿区，已经过中国社科院考古所与当地文物考古部门的发掘。采集的标本以黑釉、酱釉为主，器物有罐、碗、盘，很多黑、酱釉碗、盘饰有两道弦纹，是该窑的特点。

回民巷窑，窑址位于灵武市磁窑堡镇回民巷村西侧的瓦渣梁上，距磁窑堡镇 4 公里。窑址堆积面积不小，采集的标本主要有白釉、黑釉、酱釉、褐釉等品种。白釉器物以碗为主，采用刮圈叠烧，碗心留有涩圈。胎质较脆。有少量带装饰的器物，如白釉划花鱼纹盆等；黑釉器物有玉壶春瓶、双耳罐、壶等，肩腹部出棱的小罐较有特色。褐釉也有带印花装饰的碗。

Lingwu Kiln

The Ciyaobao kiln is located at coal district, and was excavated by the Archaeology Institution of Chinese Academy of Social Sciences and local department of cultural relic and archaeology. With black glaze and brown glaze as the main product, the collected specimen included the type of jar, bowl and plate. Some bowls and plates with two strings design were the characteristic wares of the kiln.

The Huiminxiang kiln is located at Wazhaliang, west of Huiminxiang Village of Ciyaobao Town in Lingwu, Ningxia Hui Autonomous Region. The kiln site is about 35km from the downtown of Lingwu, and 4km south of Ciyaobao Town. The heritage was not small and the collected specimen included white glaze, black glaze, brown glaze, light brown glaze, etc. With bowl as its mainstream in white glaze, the ware has a circle without glaze at inner bottom due to firing method. The body was a little tender, and some wares were decorated with pattern such as white glaze basin with incised fish design. The black glaze ware contained vase, jar with two handles, pot and so on, and the jar with outstanding shoulder was the characteristic one. The brown glaze bowl also decorated with stamped design.

灵武磁窑堡窑遗址
The heritage of Ciyaobao kiln of Lingwu

灵武磁窑堡窑遗址瓷片遗存
The porcelain shred accumulation of Ciyaobao kiln of Lingwu

260　**西夏　白釉碗标本**

Western Xia

Specimens of white glaze bowl

261 西夏 白釉碗标本

Western Xia

Specimen of white glaze bowl

附图

西夏 白釉碗

高 6.2 厘米 口径 15.5 厘米

足径 5 厘米

磁窑堡窑遗址出土

故宫博物院藏

Illustration

Western Xia White glaze bowl

Height 6.2cm, mouth diameter 15.5cm, foot diameter 5cm

Excavated at Ciyaobao kiln and collection of the Palace Museum

碗敞口，深腹，圈足。胎质较细，施化妆土，里满釉，外施釉不到底。

白瓷是磁窑堡窑生产的主要釉色品种之一，出土标本多为民用的盘、碗类器，胎质一般较粗，为掩盖较差的胎色常施化妆土再罩釉烧成，器外壁施釉多不到底，且施釉工艺相对比较粗放。此碗外施半截釉，釉层较薄，釉面流淌，施釉工艺相对比较随意。

262　**西夏　白釉碗标本**

Western Xia

Specimens of white glaze bowl

263 **西夏　白釉盆标本**

Western Xia

Specimen of white glaze basin

264　**西夏　白釉划花瓶标本**

Western Xia

Specimen of white glaze vase with incised design

附图

西夏　白釉剔划花折枝牡丹纹瓶

残高 25.5 厘米
磁窑堡窑遗址出土

Illustration
Western Xia　White glaze vase with incised and engraved peony design

Remain height 25.5cm
Excavated at Ciyaobao kiln

此器为复原的白釉剔刻花瓶。瓶敞口外卷，短直颈，折肩，深直腹，平底。胎色灰白，胎面敷化妆土并施透明釉，外壁剔刻花装饰，剔刻刀工劲健有力，腹壁菱形开光内饰折枝牡丹纹，纹样之外的部分剔掉化妆土露出胎体的本色，开光外则保留了化妆土层并在其上刻划出复线纹及浪花纹，棕褐色的胎色与施白色化妆土后形成的洁白釉面对比鲜明。

265　**西夏　白釉划花罐标本**

Western Xia

Specimen of white glaze jar with incised design

266 西夏 白釉剔花罐标本

Western Xia Specimen of white glaze jar with engraved design

附图

西夏 白釉剔花牡丹纹大罐

残高 30.4 厘米
磁窑堡窑遗址出土

Illustration
Western Xia White glaze jar with engraved peony design

Remain height 30.4cm
Excavated at Ciyaobao kiln

此器为复原的西夏瓷。罐敞口微外卷，短颈，溜肩，肩以下渐敛至底。胎质较细，胎色灰白，胎面敷化妆土并施白釉，外壁剔刻花分层装饰，肩饰莲瓣纹，腹饰缠枝牡丹纹，腹下部饰卷草纹。

剔花装饰是磁窑堡窑西夏瓷流行的装饰技法之一，从工艺特点上看，是先施化妆土刻划出花纹，再剔掉纹饰之外的化妆土露出胎体，使得纹饰突出于器表，有浅浮雕的装饰效果；再罩透明釉烧成。装饰方法都是利用较深的胎色与釉色或与比较洁白的化妆土色所形成的鲜明色差来突出纹样的装饰效果。此器腹部主题纹饰部分采用剔花工艺。

267
西夏　里白釉点彩外黑釉碗标本
Western Xia　Specimen of bowl with white glaze and spots inside and black glaze outside

268　**西夏　黑釉瓶标本**
Western Xia
Specimens of black glaze vase

附图

西夏 黑釉剔花折枝牡丹纹瓶

高 38 厘米　口径 5 厘米
足径 10 厘米
故宫博物院藏

Illustration

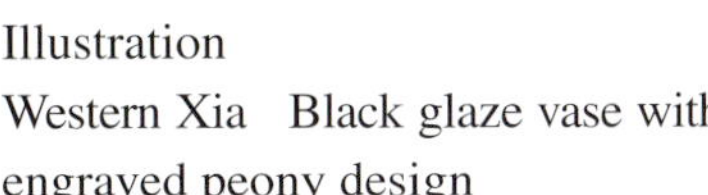
Western Xia　Black glaze vase with engraved peony design

Height 38cm, mouth diameter 5cm,
foot diameter 10cm
Collection of the Palace Museum

瓶梯形小口，短颈，折肩，长弧腹，圈足。通体施黑釉，釉色漆黑光亮，外壁剔地刻花装饰，开光内饰折枝牡丹纹。

磁窑堡窑流行的剔花装饰技法，显然深受北方，尤其是晋北地区生产磁州窑类型瓷器诸窑场的影响，与这些窑场的同类器相比，磁窑堡窑的产品剔刻花后露出的胎体面积往往较多，纹饰布局显得比较疏朗，其胎色多显浅黄或棕黄色，比晋北诸窑产品的胎色要深，胎质也显得相对粗糙。

269　西夏　黑釉双系罐标本

Western Xia

Specimens of black glaze jar with two handles

附图

西夏　黑釉双系罐

高 26.7 厘米

磁窑堡窑遗址出土

Illustration

Western Xia　Black glaze jar with two handles

Height 26.7cm

Excavated at Ciyaobao kiln

罐敛口，短颈，鼓腹，圈足。肩部饰对称的条形系。

磁窑堡窑生产的西夏瓷以白釉、黑釉、褐釉等为主，也有少量青釉、茶叶末釉瓷器，多数外施釉不到底，有些器物里外釉色不同，底足一般无釉。此罐胎质较粗，外壁施釉不到底，釉色深沉，釉面莹亮，是窑址出土的代表性器物。

270 **西夏 黑釉双系罐标本**
Western Xia Specimen of black glaze jar with two handles

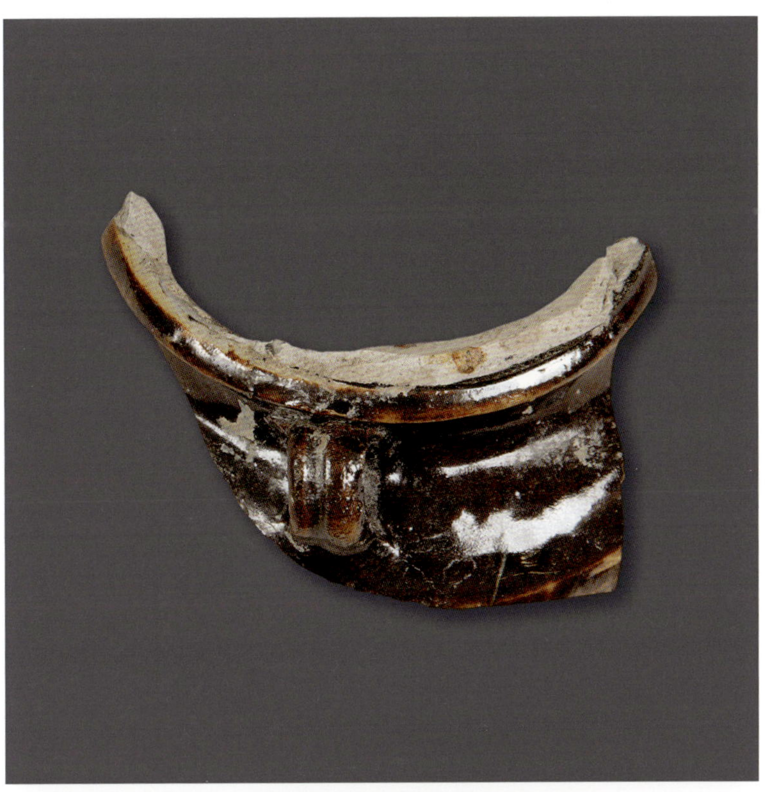

271 **西夏 黑釉罐标本**
Western Xia Specimen of black glaze jar

272　**西夏　黑釉罐标本**

Western Xia

Specimens of black glaze jar

273　西夏　黑釉碗标本
Western Xia
Specimens of black glaze bowl

274　西夏　黑釉碗标本

Western Xia

Specimens of black glaze bowl

275 **西夏 黑釉弦纹碗标本**

Western Xia

Specimen of black glaze bowl with string design

附图

西夏 褐釉刻字弦纹碗

高 8.4 厘米

Illustration

Western Xia Brown glaze bowl with string design and characters

Height 8.4cm

碗口微敛，弧壁斜收，圈足。通体施褐色釉，外施釉不到底，里施釉并刻一西夏文字。

磁窑堡窑址出土的大量盘、碗类民用瓷器采用的装烧方法有支钉支烧、支圈正烧和匣钵正烧等几种。此碗采用的是支圈正烧法，碗里心有一圈宽阔的涩胎支烧痕。此外磁窑堡窑址出土物中发现了为数不少的墨书西夏文或带西夏纪年的瓷片标本，是研究西夏文字的珍贵资料。

276 西夏 黑釉弦纹碗标本

Western Xia

Specimens of black glaze bowl with string design

277 **西夏 黑褐釉罐标本**
Western Xia
Specimen of dark brwon glaze jar

附图

西夏 黑褐釉小罐

高 4.5 厘米
磁窑堡窑遗址出土

Illustration
Western Xia Black glaze jar

Height 4.5cm
Excvated at kiln of Ciyaobao

罐敞口，短颈，折肩，深腹，腹下斜收，平底。胎质较粗。外壁所施黑釉虽然漆黑明亮，但施釉工艺显得比较随意，釉不到底且沾染大块釉斑，反映了磁窑堡窑一般民用产品制作工艺比较粗放的特色。

278　西夏　茶叶末釉双系罐标本
Western Xia
Specimens of tea-dust glaze jar with two handles

279　西夏　酱釉罐标本
Western Xia
Specimens of dark reddish brown glaze jar

280　**西夏　窑具标本**
Western Xia
Specimens of kiln furniture

281　**西夏　窑具标本**
Western Xia
Specimen of kiln furniture

灵武回民巷窑遗址
The heritage of Huiminxiang kiln in Lingwu

灵武回民巷窑遗址瓷片遗存
The porcelain shred accumulation of Huiminxiang kiln in Lingwu

282　**西夏　白釉瓶标本**
Western Xia
Specimen of white glaze vase

283　**西夏　白釉炉标本**
Western Xia
Specimen of white glaze burner

284 **西夏 白釉碗标本**

Western Xia

Specimens of white glaze bowl

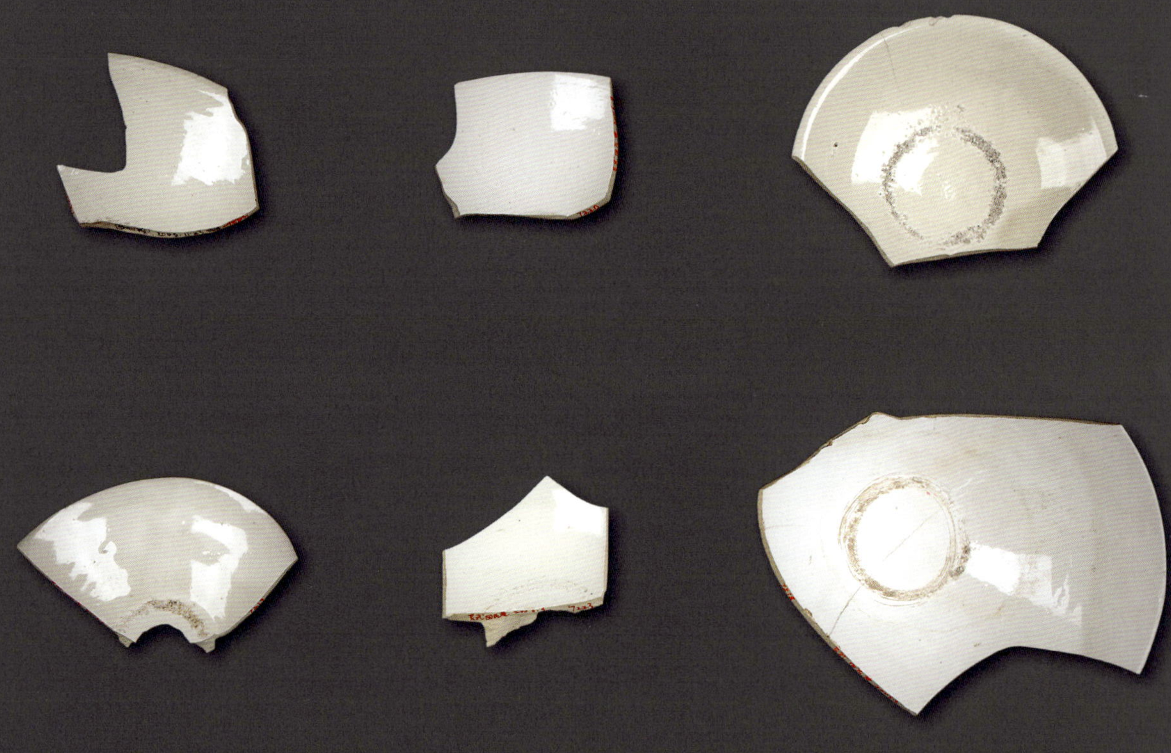

285　**西夏　白釉碗标本**

Western Xia

Specimens of white glaze bowl

286　**西夏　白釉碗标本**
Western Xia
Specimens of white glaze bowl

287 **西夏　白釉碗标本**
Western Xia
Specimens of white glaze bowl

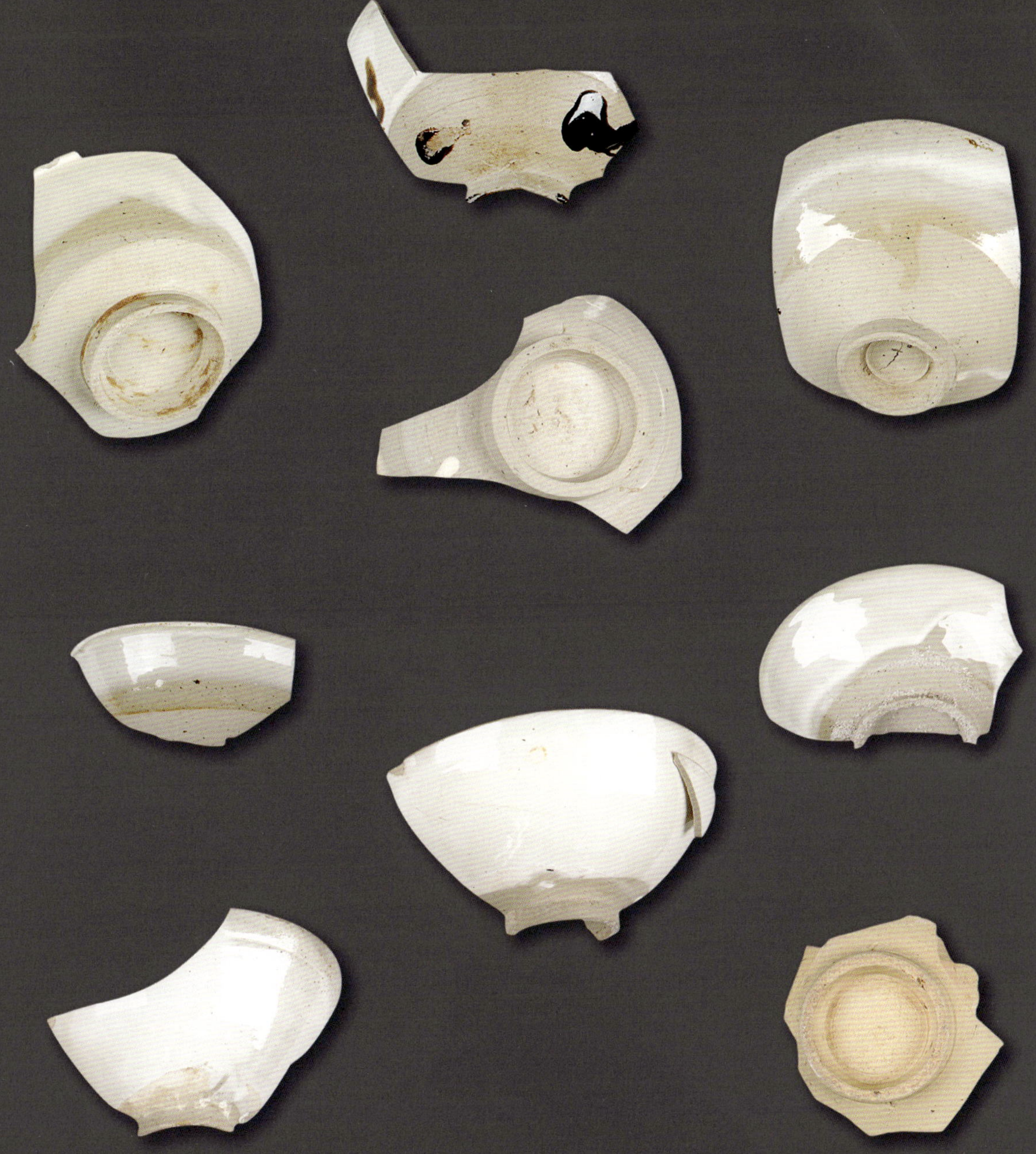

288 **西夏　白釉盘标本**
Western Xia
Specimen of white glaze plate

289 **西夏　白釉划花枕标本**
Western Xia Specimens of white glaze pillow with incised design

290 **西夏　里白釉划花外黑褐釉盆标本**

Western Xia

Specimens of white glaze basin with incised design inside and dark brown glaze outside

291　西夏　里白釉点彩外黑褐釉盆标本

Western Xia

Specimens of white glaze basin with spots inside and dark brown glaze outside

292 西夏 里白釉外酱釉盆标本

Western Xia

Specimens of white glaze basin inside and dark reddish brown glaze outside

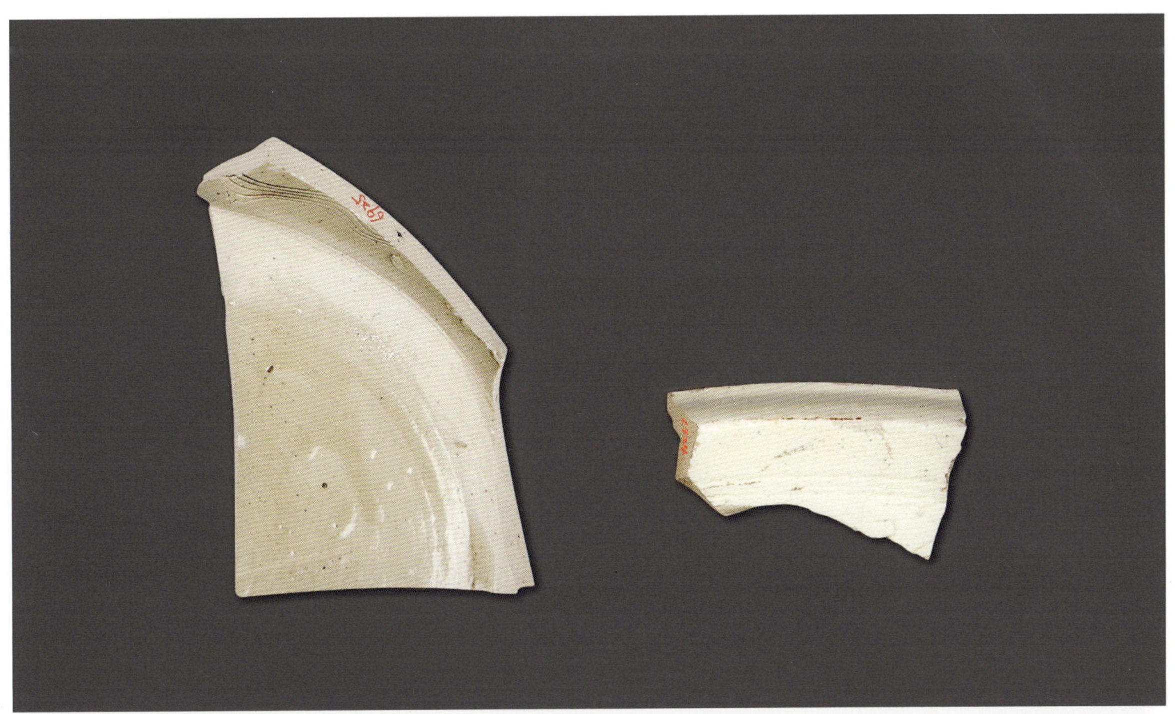

293　**西夏　黑釉瓶标本**

Western Xia

Specimens of black glaze vase

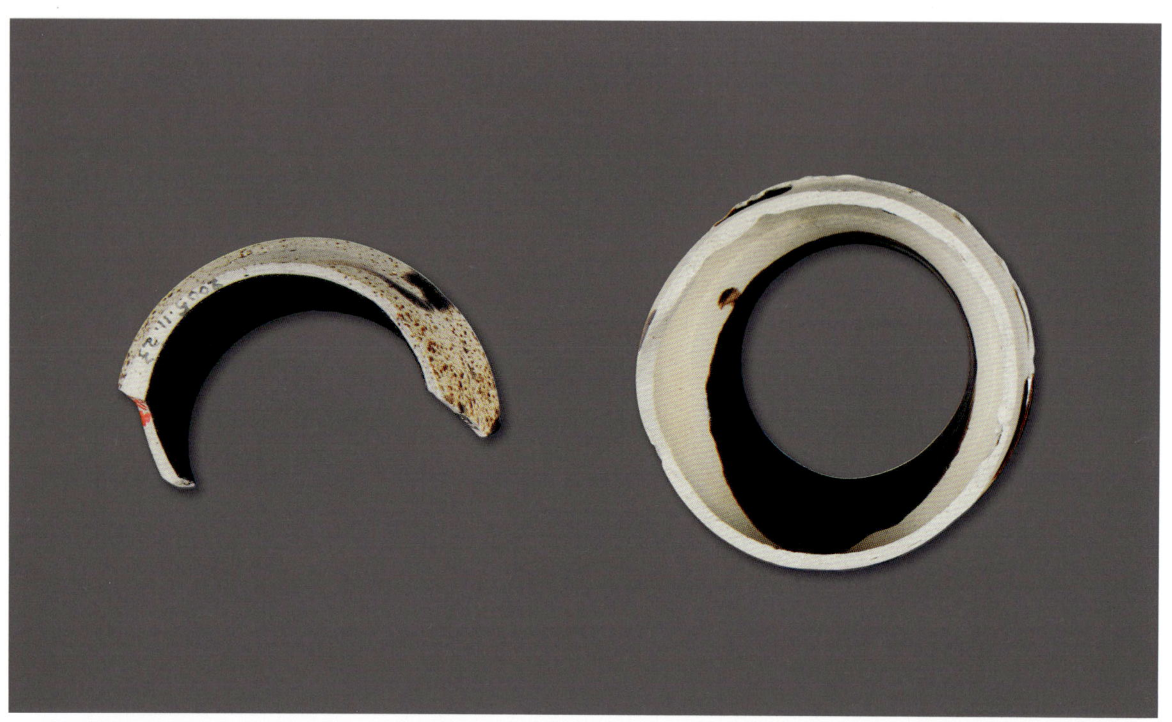

294　**西夏　黑釉双系罐标本**
Western Xia
Specimens of black glaze jar with two handles

295 西夏 黑釉罐标本
Western Xia
Specimens of black glaze jar

296 西夏 黑釉壶标本
Western Xia
Specimen of black glaze pot

297 **西夏 黑釉器盖标本**
Western Xia Specimens of black glaze cover

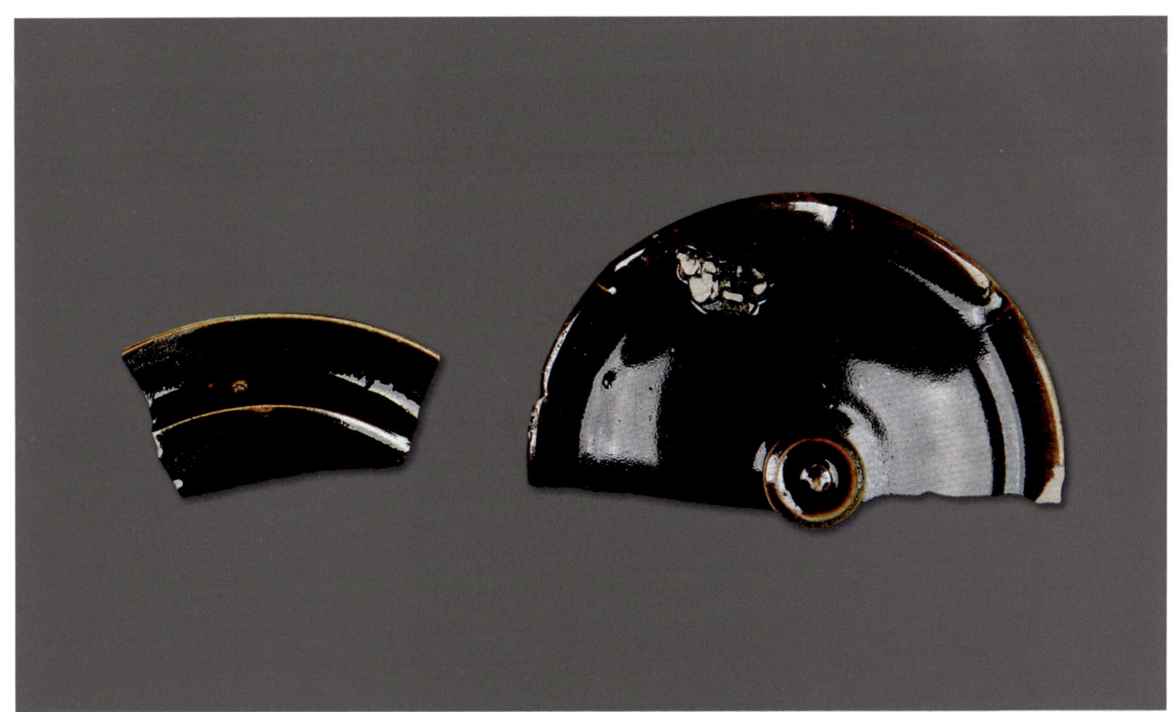

298 西夏 黑釉碗标本
Western Xia Specimens of black glaze bowl

299 西夏 黑釉碗标本
Western Xia
Specimens of black glaze bowl

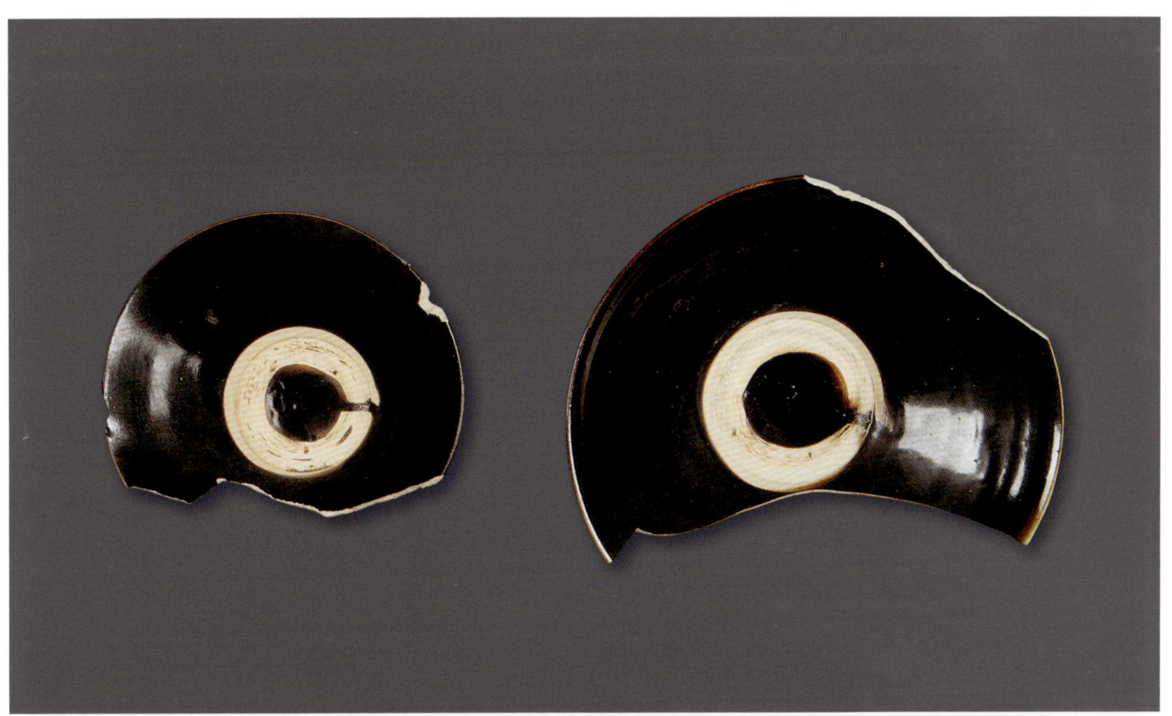

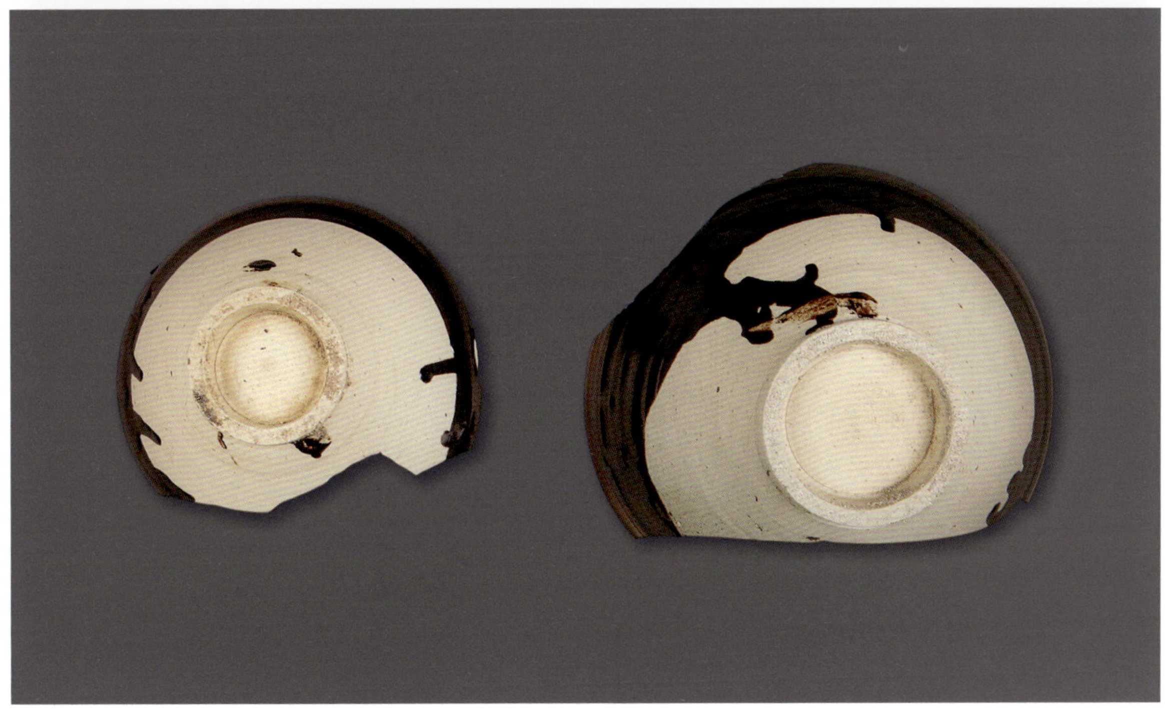

300
西夏　褐釉双系罐标本
Western Xia
Specimen of brown glaze jar with two handles

301
西夏　茶叶末釉碗标本
Western Xia
Specimens of tea-dust glaze bowl

302　**西夏　茶叶末釉碗标本**
Western Xia
Specimen of tea-dust glaze bowl

303　**西夏　酱釉双系罐标本**
Western Xia
Specimen of dark reddish brown glaze jar with two handles

304　**西夏　酱釉盒标本**
Western Xia
Specimen of dark reddish brown glaze box

305 西夏 酱釉印花花卉纹碗标本

Western Xia

Specimens of dark reddish brown glaze bowl with stamped floral design

306 **西夏　酱釉刻线纹碗标本**
Western Xia　Specimen of dark reddish brown glaze bowl with carved string design

307 **西夏　窑具标本**
Western Xia
Specimens of kiln furniture

辽宁

辽宁省目前已发现的窑址数量不多，辽阳江官屯窑是一处较有代表性的辽代瓷窑。

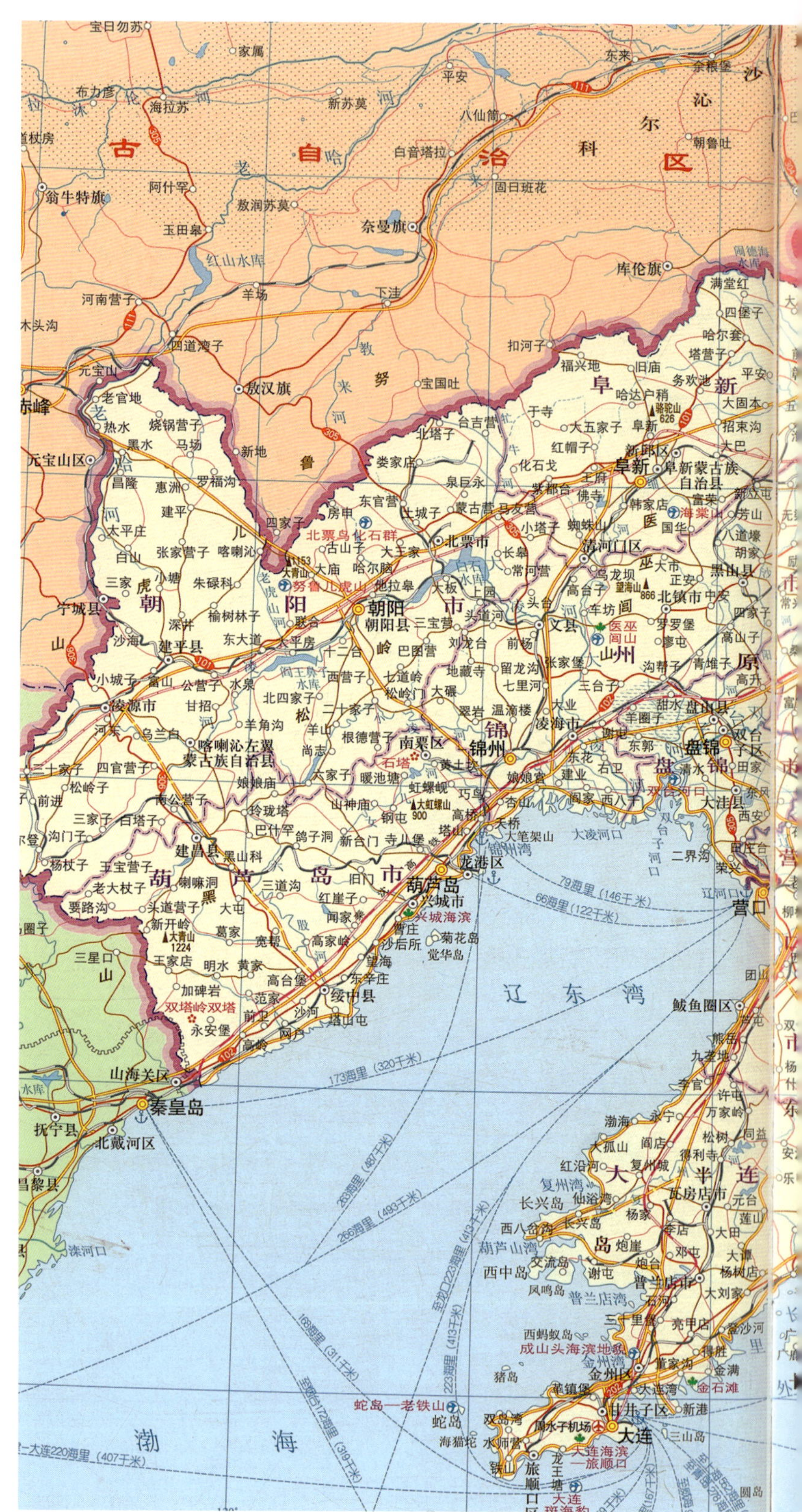

辽宁窑址分布图

Liaoning Province

The kilns in Liaoning Province were less in number at present, and one of the weighted kilns of Liao dynasty is Guantun kiln of Liaoyang.

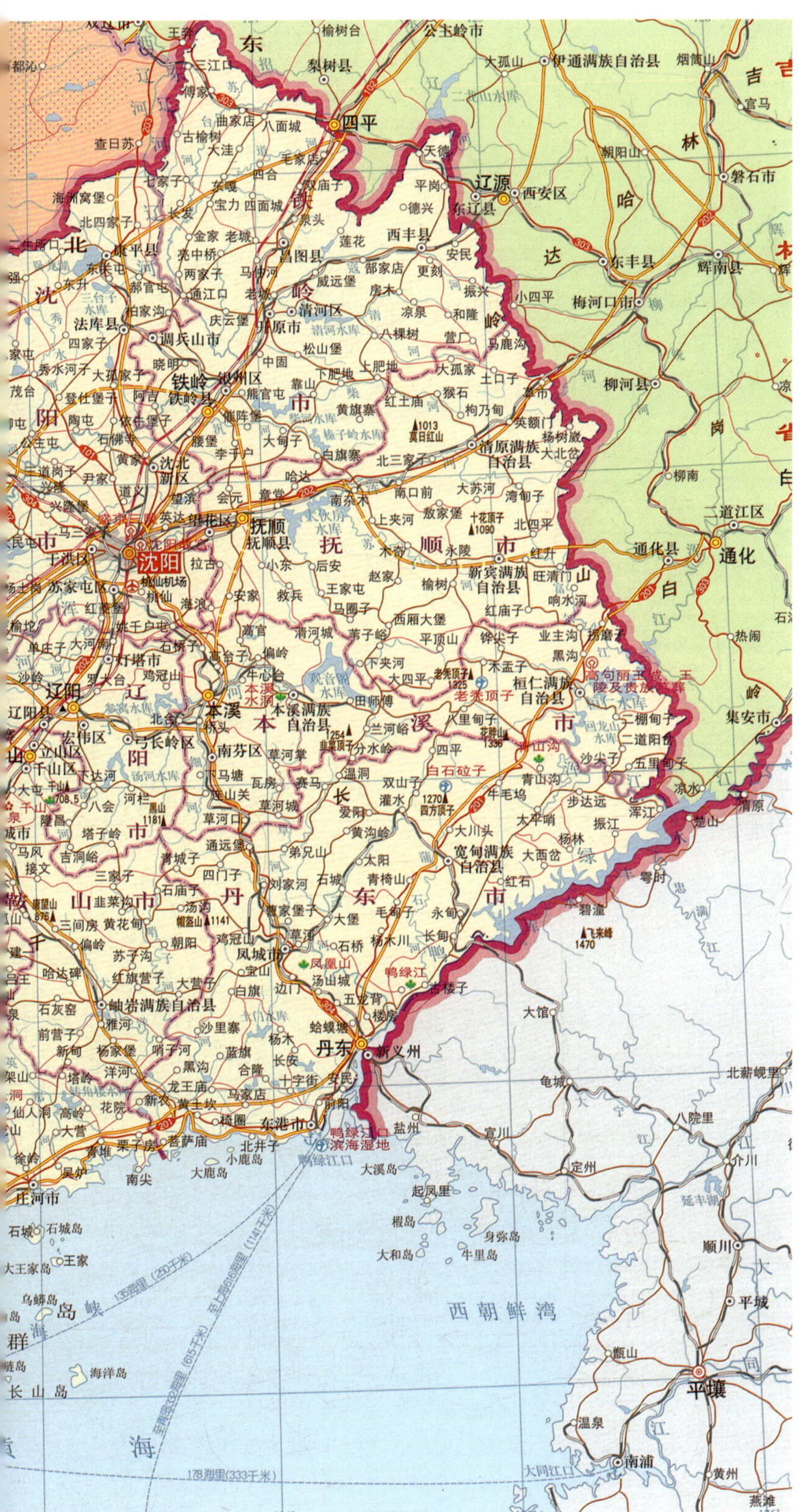

The Distribution Map of Kilns in Liaoning Province

辽阳窑

窑址位于辽阳市东南方向江官屯村，太子河沿岸。辽代瓷窑。2006年故宫博物院的部分专家学者对该瓷窑进行了调查。窑址瓷片堆积还比较丰富。主要品种有白釉、白地褐花、白地黑花、黑釉、酱釉等。白釉器物有碗、盘、罐、缸、器盖等；白地黑花器物有花卉纹碗、器盖；黑釉器物有碗、罐、瓶、壶等，有些碗上有酱色兔毫纹，制作比较精细；酱釉器釉质匀净，有些泛红色，器形有碗、瓶、罐及小动物，有些薄胎小件器物制作比较精细。总体上看，该窑多数器物胎质比较粗糙。

Liaoyang Kiln

The kiln is located at southeast of Jiangguantun Village in Liaoyang and nearby the Taizi river. The kiln belonged to Liao dynasty was one of the kilns. The ceramic experts and scholars of the Palace Museum investigated the kiln in 2006. The porcelain specimens were rich in number, including white glaze, brown color on white ground, black color on white ground, black glaze, brown glaze, etc. The white glaze ware contained bowl, plate, jar, vat, cover, etc. The black color on white ground ware included bowl with floral design and cover. The black glaze ware included bowl, jar, vase, pot, and some bowls with brown hare's fure glaze was in delicate look. The brown glaze ware has pure glaze, and some turned glossy red. The type of brown glaze included bowl, vase, jar and animal-shaped toy, and some small ware with thin body was fine in quality. In general, most of wares in the kiln were rough in body.

辽阳窑遗址（太子河沿岸）
The heritage of Liaoyang kiln (near the Taizi river)

辽阳窑遗址瓷片遗存
The porcelain shred accumulation of Liaoyang kiln

辽阳窑遗址瓷片遗存
The porcelain shred accumulation of Liaoyang kiln

308 辽 白釉瓶标本
Liao dynasty
Specimen of white glaze vase

309 辽 白釉碗标本
Liao dynasty
Specimen of white glaze bowl

310　辽　白釉碗标本
Liao dynasty
Specimens of white glaze bowl

311　辽　白釉碗标本

Liao dynasty

Specimens of white glaze bowl

312　**辽　白釉盘标本**

Liao dynasty

Specimens of white glaze plate

313　辽　白釉划花罐盖标本
Liao dynasty
Specimen of white glaze jar cover with incised design

314　辽　白地褐花罐标本
Liao dynasty
Specimen of white glaze jar with brown color

315　辽　白地褐花碗标本
Liao dynasty
Specimen of white glaze bowl with brown color

316　辽　里酱釉外白釉盒标本

Liao dynasty　Specimen of box with dark reddish brown glaze inside and white glaze outside

317　辽　青褐釉瓶标本

Liao dynasty　Specimen of celadon vase

318　**辽　黑釉碗标本**

Liao dynasty

Specimens of black glaze bowl

319　**辽　黑釉碗标本**

Liao dynasty

Specimens of black glaze bowl

320　辽　酱釉双系瓶标本
Liao dynasty
Specimen of dark reddish brown glaze vase with two handles

321　辽　酱釉瓶标本
Liao dynasty
Specimen of dark reddish brown glaze vase

322　辽　酱釉双系罐标本
Liao dynasty
Specimen of dark reddish brown glaze jar with two handles

323　**辽　酱釉罐标本**

Liao dynasty

Specimens of dark reddish brown glaze jar

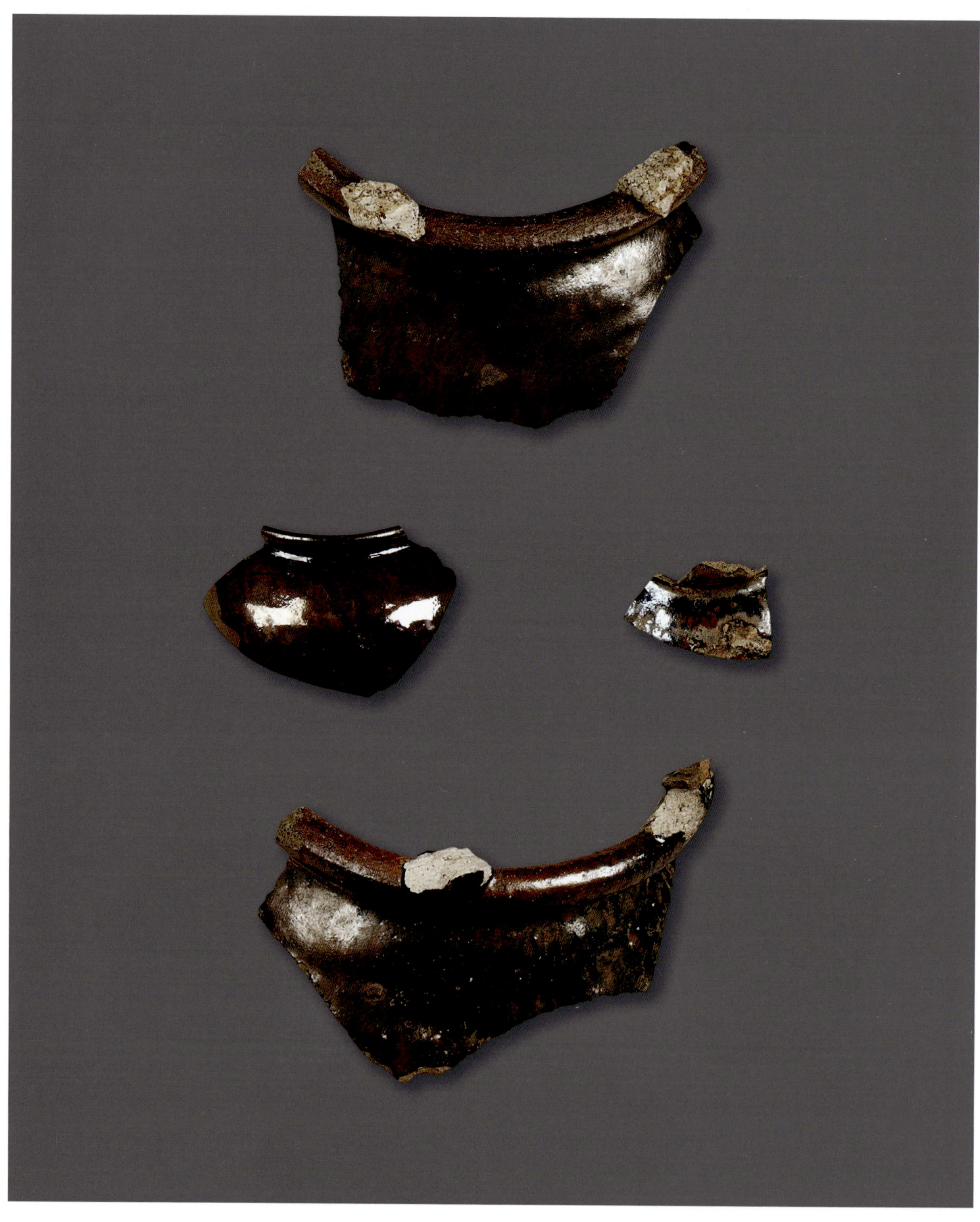

324　**辽　酱釉碗标本**

Liao dynasty

Specimens of dark reddish brown glaze bowl

325　辽　酱釉碗标本

Liao dynasty

Specimens of dark reddish brown glaze bowl

326　**辽　酱釉小马标本**

Liao dynasty

Specimen of dark reddish brown glaze horse

窑址考察论文选

Selected Thesis on Kiln Investigation

山东淄博磁村窑址调查

董健丽

山东磁窑村窑址位于淄博市淄川区西南10公里，窑址面积较大，村东、村内至村南两公里的范围内均有分布，为山东古代一处重要的民窑。窑址分为四区：南北窑洼区、村内区、华严寺区和苹果园区。据文献记载，磁村窑始烧于唐，一直延续到金、元，制瓷历史悠久，产品种类丰富。北宋时期，官府在磁村窑设官收税，证明当时烧制瓷器的规模和产业的兴隆景况。金代磁村窑瓷器生产规模较北宋时期有较大发展。磁村窑明以前称"磁窑务"，《淄川县志》记载："……磁窑务，县西二十五"[1]。1976年10月山东省博物馆、淄博市博物馆、淄博市陶瓷工业公司和宁阳县文化馆对此窑遗址试掘，同年12月，故宫博物院古陶瓷工作者对其又进行了调查。2006年10月，故宫博物院再次对磁村窑址进行调查。笔者根据两次调查采集的瓷片标本，结合墓葬出土的磁村窑瓷器，谈谈对该窑瓷器的初步认识。

一 主要器类

两次共采集的标本约300件，器类分为碗、盘、盆、缸、钵、壶、瓶、罐、炉和铃等。碗类是该窑生产最多的品种，各类碗可能要占该窑采集产品总数的70%以上。依据器形磁村窑器物分以下几类：

1．碗类

分为八式：

I式。平底，底心微凹入，灰色胎，含黑色杂质，胎粗而厚重，碗内施青绿色釉，碗心积釉处有2个支钉痕，胎厚0.6厘米。

II式。口撇，玉璧底，器腹较深，碗内心有很大的支钉痕。胎浅砖红色，胎略重，敷白色化妆土，白釉上点绿彩，绿彩浓翠。高16厘米，口径13厘米，底径8厘米。

Ⅲ式。侈口，翻沿，圆唇，曲腹，圈足，足墙略厚。土黄色胎，碗内外施满酱色釉，釉色发红。高10厘米，足径6厘米。

Ⅳ式。撇口，矮圈足，深腹，白色胎，胎体轻薄，芒口无釉，涂酱口，通体施白釉，釉色银白，碗心刮釉一周。高9厘米，口径12厘米，足径7厘米。

Ⅴ式。白胎，圈足，施乳白色釉，外壁施釉到口沿。碗内一种有纤细的印花，并有支钉痕；另一种内壁刻划枝叶纹，碗心刮圈，胎厚 0.6 厘米。

Ⅵ式。侈口，口沿微敞，窄圈足。白胎较薄。施黑釉，漆黑光亮，品质极高。胎壁 0.3 厘米。

Ⅶ式。直口，弧腹，平底微凹，足上有三个圆点痕。白胎，器内施黑釉，器外施釉到口沿，足径 7 厘米。

Ⅷ式。敞口，弧腹，碗心坦平。圈足微撇，挖足深。土黄色胎，施青黄釉，内壁印缠枝菊，碗心刮圈。高 4 厘米，口径 9 厘米，足径 2.5 厘米。

2．盘类

分为三式：

Ⅰ式。敞口，直腹，圈足。白胎，施黑釉，釉色均匀而光亮，盘心有长形支钉痕。高 7 厘米，足径 5 厘米。

Ⅱ式。敛口，弧腹，圈足。土黄色胎，胎质坚致而细腻，施棕黄色釉，盘心无釉露胎，盘内壁印缠枝花纹。高 7 厘米，口径 15 厘米，足径 6 厘米。

Ⅲ式。直口，圈足，白胎，施茶叶末色釉。足径 7 厘米。

3．壶类

分为二式：

Ⅰ式。花式，斜流，胎土黄色，施黑釉，口边露出青黄色。口径 5.5 厘米。

Ⅱ式。口微撇，粗颈，溜肩，其上有一斜出短流。土黄色胎，施黑釉，口边露青黄色。流长 3.5 厘米。

4．罐类

分为七式：

Ⅰ式。口微敛，系为三个条状并列在一起。土黄色胎，施乳白釉，施釉较薄，胎厚 0.5 厘米。

Ⅱ式。口略撇，短颈肩腹之间有一双泥条系。灰胎，施黑釉，其上有不规则的铁锈红斑，胎厚 0.6 厘米。

Ⅲ式。直口，土黄色胎，施象牙白色釉，罐身刻划较深的竖条纹，露胎，胎厚 0.6 厘米。

Ⅳ式。土黄色胎，敷化妆土，其上施乳白色釉，剔刻回纹边饰，露出粉色化妆土，胎厚 0.5 厘米。

Ⅴ式。直口，白胎，施黑釉，口边露酱色。器腹有等距离的白色凸线纹，另外还有三条一组凸线、四条一组的白色凸线纹、六条一组酱色凸线和有十条一组凸线纹。胎厚 0.6 厘米。

Ⅵ式。唇口，土黄色胎，白釉绘水波纹，另外还有花叶纹、竹叶纹、卷草纹等。胎厚 1 厘米。

Ⅶ式。土黄色胎，施褐色釉，颈部有两道弦纹，器腹布满戳印纹，胎厚 0.5 厘米。

5．钵类

敛口，弧腹，口沿贴水波纹一周。口沿施青褐色釉，器身无釉，露胎，胎厚 0.5 厘米。

6．瓶类

身体瘦长，近底渐收，撇足。灰胎，胎质细腻，施黑釉，釉色均匀。足径 6 厘米。

7．灯类

折沿，深腹，壁身垂直，白胎，施白釉。器身长 6 厘米。

8．盒类

圆形，子母口，白釉地上划出三道弦纹，内刻划长点纹。口径 11 厘米。

9．盆类

缸胎，胎粗而厚重，用白釉黑花为饰，有花卉纹、竹叶纹、卷草纹和弦纹等。胎厚 1 ~ 1.5 厘米。

10．铃类

上小下大，弧腹，最上部施少许黑釉，其下大部分施白釉。器物小巧，最大径 5 厘米。

二 釉色品种

根据采集的标本，磁村窑釉色可分为青釉、茶叶末釉、酱釉、白釉、白釉绿斑、黑釉、棕黄釉、翠蓝釉和白地黑花 9 个品种。其中以白釉、黑釉和褐釉为主，青釉和白地黑花次之，而白釉划花、白釉剔花和翠蓝釉等很少。

1．青釉

釉色分黄绿、青灰和青褐色。有的施釉不均匀，有的在碗的中心有较厚的积釉现象，数量不多。

2．茶叶末釉

颜色就像茶叶的碎末聚集在一起，釉面不光亮，但较典雅。这种釉本来是为了烧黑釉而配制的，由于烧成温度和火焰气氛的关系而烧成了茶叶末的颜色。此次采集的标本不多，见盘和罐等器物。

3．酱色釉

釉面像芝麻酱的褐色，有两种颜色，一种发红，一种为“紫定”，其胎体极薄，施釉光亮。

4．白釉

是该窑生产的主要品种。磁村窑的白釉又分两种：一是银白色釉，釉光莹润，在胎体上施洁白的化妆土，加之釉质细腻，白釉的质量很高；一是象牙白釉，白釉略泛黄，釉层和胎体之间施白色化妆土，类似定窑的象牙白釉，也是磁村窑质量较好的作品。

5．白釉绿斑

首创于晚唐北方窑场，是磁村窑的常见品种，白釉发黄，绿斑浓翠，用在陶胎、灰胎和土黄胎器物上。

6．黑釉

磁村窑黑瓷生产数量与白瓷差不多，属于大宗产品。依釉色又可细分 5 种：

第一种，黑釉非常细腻，釉色均匀，光泽度高，没有流釉和积釉现象，用在白胎薄胎器上，是黑釉瓷的极品。

第二种，黑中发褐，釉层较薄，在高温中釉层被胎面的孔隙吸收，釉面出现许多橘皮棕眼，釉层不均匀，用在胎体略厚的灰胎器上。

第三种，黑釉凝厚而光亮，在器物的口沿出现天蓝色的窑变现象。施在土黄色胎上。

第四种，黑釉较黑，釉面上散布着许多银色金属光泽的小圆点，大小不一，大的直径达数毫米，小的只有针尖大小，形似油滴，用在土黄色胎和灰胎器物上。

第五种，黑釉光亮，用含铁量较高的彩料直接绘于黑釉的釉面之上，烧成后在漆黑光亮的釉面上可见美丽的铁锈“斑花”。

7．棕黄釉

外观接近青瓷，大多数是棕黄色、黄绿色和褐绿色，用在土黄胎的印花器物上[2]。

8．翠蓝釉

是一种低温釉，有的学者称之为“孔雀绿”，亦称之为“翡翠釉”，用在土黄色胎上。

9．白地黑花

即在成型的坯上，先敷一层洁白的化妆土，然后用细黑料绘制纹样，再施一层薄而透明的玻璃釉。这类作品大多用在缸胎粗瓷上。

三 重要品种

此次又采集到一些重要的釉色品种瓷片，所谓重要品种有两层含义：一层是指与邻省窑口的品种相似，但装饰手法和纹饰题材有“新意”；另一层是指传统观念认为的只有河北、河南等省有的品种——白地黑花和白釉剔花。通过对山东淄博磁村窑的发掘和调查，发现了该窑也有生产，从而纠正了我们传统认识，是一种“新发现”。

1．紫定

即文献中所指的“色柴”，其釉色与今天的芝麻酱色很相近，着色剂为氧化铁。宋代河北定窑、陕西耀州窑、河南修武窑和江西吉州窑都有该品种。此次采集的一小片磁村窑标本，其胎质比定窑“紫定”还要细腻，且胎体特薄，釉色匀净。

2．白釉划花

一般在白釉碗、盘内划满花卉，衬以篦划纹，纹样均衡对称，是河北磁州窑、定窑，河南鹤壁窑、扒村窑等常见的装饰方法。此次采集的一件磁村窑白釉划花不同上述各窑所使用的传统的均衡对称装饰技法，而用不对称的手法在碗内壁刻划两枝折枝花叶蜿蜒伸出碗壁，摇曳多姿。

3．黑釉贴双环纹

所谓贴花，是把各种图案做成浮雕状，然后贴在器皿上。磁村窑采集到的黑釉贴花双环纹罐，纹样十分醒目而夸张，为其他窑所罕见。

4．黑釉凸线纹

黑釉凸线纹是在黑釉的胎上用泥堆起直线纹，又称“粉杠”，河北磁州窑，河南的汤阴、密县、登封、禹县、宝丰和鲁山等窑口都有生产，磁村窑的凸线纹不同上述各窑，立体感强，布局多种多样，而且种类特别丰富。

5．棕黄釉印花

棕黄釉印花器外观接近青瓷，大多数是棕黄色、黄绿色和褐绿色，用印花装饰器物，这类品种在陕西铜川黄堡窑址晚唐地层中就有出土。此外河北磁州窑，山西介休窑、榆次窑和陕西旬邑窑也曾有出土。从此次采集的 5 件磁村窑棕黄釉印花盘、碗看，该窑也烧制这类产品，且花纹精致，除上述窑常见的花卉纹外，还新创了鱼纹、凤凰纹等。

6．翠蓝釉加紫刻花

该釉在山西发现很多，河北磁州窑和河南扒村窑也有烧造。磁村窑有单色翠蓝釉和翠蓝釉加紫刻花品种。

7．绞胎

绞胎唐代兴起，日常器类有碗、盘、杯、瓶、钵、枕和炉等。绞胎瓷最早在陕西铜川耀州窑唐代地层出土，宋代河南的当阳峪、宝丰清凉寺和新安窑等烧制。在磁村窑第五期金元地层中出土了绞胎球，素胎，为黑和白两色胎泥绞制而成，这种绞胎球从现有的材料看仅见磁村窑烧造。故宫近年收藏了 6 个大小和色彩不同的绞胎球，其中白黑绞胎球，应为磁村窑产品。

8．白地黑花

白釉黑花器物是磁州窑创烧，并广泛地影响到中原地区的很多瓷窑，形成了北方民间瓷器的主流。目前公私收藏的白地黑花盆类器通常被判定为河南鹤壁、郏县和禹县扒村等窑口生产。此次故宫在磁村窑采集了 21 件白地黑花盆，表明该窑也生产这类产品。

9．白釉剔花

白釉剔花是首先在器物胎体上施釉或施化妆土，并刻出花纹，然后将花纹部分或纹样以外的釉层或化妆土层剔去，露出胎体，然后罩以透明釉。器物烧成后，釉色、化妆土色与胎地形成强烈对比。这类品种通常归到河南修武当阳峪窑和河北磁州窑。从采集的磁村窑剔花回纹边饰样本看，该窑也生产这类产品。

四 装饰特征

从采集的标本分析，磁村窑瓷器有胎装饰、釉装饰和白地黑花三种装饰方法。

1. 胎装饰

有刻划花、印花、剔花、戳印和凸线纹等。

刻划花主要用来装饰白釉器，以花卉纹做纹样。采集的磁村窑白釉刻划折枝花，纹样的设计突破了传统的几何形图案，追求自由奔放灵动的美感，可谓设计独特，技艺精湛。印花是用刻有装饰纹样的瓷质印模，在尚未干透的瓷胎上拍印出花纹；或用刻有纹样的模子制坯，直接在瓷坯上留下花纹。磁村窑的印花用在棕黄釉器上，用缠枝花、水波游鱼和凤纹做装饰，做工很精致。凸线纹多用在黑釉上，凸线布局多种多样，用每三条一组、四条一组、六条一组、十条一组和等距离的凸线纹装饰器腹，用在碗、罐、执壶和花式瓶上。黑釉凸线（粉杠）是磁村窑代表性作品。

2. 釉装饰

有黑釉、黑釉铁锈红、油滴釉、白釉黑边和翠蓝釉，主要用在黑釉器上，采集有油滴釉和黑釉铁锈红釉。

磁村窑的黑釉油滴釉随光线的不同而变化，似群星闪烁。磁村窑的黑釉铁锈红，其黑釉十分光亮，铁锈红斑纹如行云流水自然天成，黑红对比具有沉着浑厚的美感，这类瓷器有碗、罐、壶和灯等。

3. 白地黑花瓷

用黑或黑褐两色施彩，黑彩有浓淡之分，题材以花叶纹、竹叶纹和波浪纹为主，运笔洒脱，线条明快，图案清晰。主要用在罐、玉壶春瓶和盆等器物上。

五 烧造时间

根据磁村窑试掘报告[3]，磁村窑烧瓷始于唐，而终于元，共分五期。第一期为唐中期，第二期为唐晚期，第三期为五代至北宋早期，第四期为北宋中晚期，第五期为金元时期。从采集的碗标本看，胎粗而厚，杂质多，釉色分黄绿、青灰、土黄、青褐和淡青色，碗内有三枚大的支钉痕，为唐代中期器物。从采集到的两件褐釉钵看，口沿有釉，器身无釉，并在口沿出现一周贴塑的水波纹，为唐代晚期或稍晚期器物。褐釉戳印纹双系罐与河北邯郸博物馆藏唐代褐釉戳印纹注壶的花纹一样，应为唐代器物。采集的白釉绿彩碗，胎浅红，白釉略发黄，碗内壁有对称的三个绿色斑点，外底无釉，有三个支钉痕，为北宋早期器物。白釉有简单的划花碗和剔花盒等，为北宋晚期产品。采集为数众多的光洁白釉、漆黑黑釉、黑釉铁锈红、黑釉凸线纹、棕黄釉印花、白釉黑口边、白釉划花、白釉黑花和翠蓝釉器等应为金代器物。从采集的标本数看，金代的标本约占总数的 90% 以上，因此金代是磁村窑烧瓷的鼎盛时期。

六 产品特点

磁村窑地处山东，与河北、河南窑口关系最为密切，烧制的釉色品种很多与河北和河南瓷窑相似，但在烧造产量、装烧工艺、纹饰、胎、釉和器物的种类上还是有很多不同之处。

1．一些釉色品种产量大、质量上乘

黑釉瓷是北方普遍烧造的品种，最早见于唐代陕西、河南和山东瓷窑。磁村窑唐代盛烧黑釉瓷器，产量较河南和陕西量大，器皿以碗最多，瓶、壶、罐、炉等次之。釉质晶莹滋润、色黑如漆，磁村窑的唐代黑釉瓷在北方黑釉瓷中可谓上品。磁村窑生产的瓷器在墓地和遗址中也多次出土。如 1986 年山东省张店沣水镇范王村唐墓出土的黑釉花式碗；1998 年山东省淄博市淄川区出土的黑釉长颈瓶[4]；2004 年山东省章丘市城角头墓地 M478 出土的唐代黑釉瓶[5]；1976 年山东省淄博市淄川区出土的宋代白釉瓜棱罐[6]；1998 年山东省造纸厂出土的宋代黑釉白边碗[7]；1987 年山东省兖州市李海村出土的金代绞胎球[8]；1996 年山东省淄博市淄川区磁村出土的金代黑釉凸线纹系罐[9]；山东省垦利出土的黑釉凸线纹罐和棕黄釉印花盘[10]等，山东省广饶出土的金代白地黑花花口瓶、黑釉凸线纹荷叶口瓶和黑釉凸线纹双系罐[11]、山东省昌乐东山元代 21 座墓葬出土的大量黑瓷罐、碗和碟[12]。其出土物分布在山东的东北、西南、中北和南部很多地区，表明磁村窑在山东是有广泛影响力的瓷窑。

2．装烧工艺不同

河北磁州窑，河南的汤阴、密县、登封、禹县、宝丰、鲁山等窑口生产的黑釉凸线纹，在胎上一般起黄线，起线较细，器内一般不施釉，或半釉，而淄博磁村窑黑釉凸线纹，起线为白色，线条粗且有立体感，器内施釉，内底刮釉，可套烧其他器物，显然与其他窑口有区别。

3．纹样丰富而精细

河北磁州窑、山西介休窑和榆次窑生产的棕黄釉印花瓷，多为缠枝牡丹、缠枝菊纹，磁村窑的这类品种除了上述窑口常见的缠枝花外，还有四鱼纹和凤穿花纹，装饰题材较上述各窑更加丰富，花纹也很精细。

4．胎、釉、彩和烧造器物种类不同

河南鹤壁、郏县和禹县扒村等窑口都烧造的白地黑花盆，从故宫博物院藏扒村窑烧造的近百件白地黑花盆标本看，扒村窑是生产这类产品的主要瓷窑，磁村窑受扒村窑影响很大，但也有不同：扒村窑胎灰色且致密，釉色洁白；磁村窑缸胎，呈浅砖红色，白釉有黄白和洁白两色。在用彩方面，扒村窑黑彩浓黑，磁村窑黑彩有浓淡之分。在器形上，扒村窑种类丰富，有碗、瓶、罐、缸、盆和枕等，磁村窑主要为盆，种类少于扒村窑。

磁村窑与山东省的其他瓷窑也有一定的关系，烧造的器物和釉色品种与这些窑口的产品十分近似。据目前已掌握的考古资料看，淄博寨里窑的青褐釉碗、褐黑釉注壶与磁村唐代中晚期一样[13]。淄博巩家务窑出土的碗、罐、瓶、盆和灯等，造型、胎骨和釉色与磁村窑的第三期、第四期同类器相同[14]。淄博坡地窑采集的碗、灯等器物的胎骨、釉色、造型均和磁村窑第四期遗物完全一致[15]。枣庄中陈郝南窑出土的玩具带钮小龟、黑釉狗、青釉马与淄博磁村窑址第二期同类器物相同；白瓷灯、白釉绿彩碗和罐与磁村窑第三期同类器物相同；白釉双系罐与第四期同类器物相同；而大量的白釉碗，其口稍敛，浅斜腹，圈足，碗底及碗心内一圈无釉，以及数量颇多的白釉黑花器物，都表现了与磁村窑第五期的一致性[16]。

七 结语

通过故宫博物院此次对磁村窑址的调查，我们基本搞清了它的面貌以及与邻省和本省诸多瓷窑的关系。磁村窑烧造的瓷器与北方广大地域内出现的装饰手法相一致，特别受毗邻的河北、河南等北方著名窑口影响，在吸收其他瓷窑制瓷技术的基础上，逐渐形成了自己的特色产品。此外，磁村窑对同处鲁西南的本地窑口也产生了很大的影响。

注释：

1（明）王琮纂修:《淄川县志》卷六，明嘉靖二十五年（1546 年）刻本。

2［日］长谷部乐尔:《磁州窑》，《陶磁大系》第 39 册，平凡社，1974 年。

3 山东淄博陶瓷史编写组:《山东淄博市淄川区磁村古窑址试掘简报》，《文物》1978 年第 6 期。

4 张柏主编:《中国出土瓷器全集》（山东）图版 89，科学出版社，2008 年。

5 张柏主编:《中国出土瓷器全集》（山东）图版 66，科学出版社，2008 年。

6 张柏主编:《中国出土瓷器全集》（山东）图版 117，科学出版社，2008 年。

7 张柏主编:《中国出土瓷器全集》（山东）图版 140，科学出版社，2008 年。

8 张柏主编:《中国出土瓷器全集》（山东）图版 72，科学出版社，2008 年。

9 张柏主编:《中国出土瓷器全集》（山东）图版 170，科学出版社，2008 年。

10 赵金:《山东垦利首次发现宋元时期文化遗址》，《中国文物报》2006 年 9 月 6 日。

11 赵金:《山东广饶出土的宋金瓷器选介》，《中国文物报》2008 年 1 月 30 日第 3 版。

12 昌乐县文物管理所:《山东昌乐东山王元代墓葬清理简报》，《考古》1995 年第 9 期。

13 文物编辑委员会编:《中国古代窑址调查发掘报告集》页 356，文物出版社，1984 年。

14 张光明、毕思良:《山东淄博窑址出土的油滴黑釉瓷器》页 836，《考古》1988 年第 9 期。

15 淄博市博物馆:《山东淄博坡地窑址的调查与试掘》，《中国古代窑址调查发掘报告集》，文物出版社，1984 年。

16 枣庄市文物管理站:《山东枣庄古窑址调查》，《中国古代窑址调查发掘报告集》，文物出版社，1984 年。

Abstract of Investigation on Cicun kiln of Zibo in Shandong Province

Dong Jianli

The Shandong area had been an important production base for porcelain in northern China since Northern Dynasties, and has achieved new progress in Sui and Tang dynasty based on the founding of over 60 kilns in this period. The kilns in Shandong area reached its peak in Song and Jin dynasty with over 10 kilns by official excavation, and Cicun kiln was a significance one. According to the ancient records, the Cicun kiln which has a long history, started its firing in Tang dynasty, and continued to Jin and Yuan dynasty. In Northern Song dynasty, the feudal official set up an institution of paying tax, and it proved the prosperous condition of porcelain making. Comparing to the Northern Song dynasty, the scale of production had expanded in Jin dynasty.The kiln site is located at the place that 10km far from southwest of Cichuan District in Zibo, and was large in scale. The antiquarian of Shandong took the tentative excavation in Oct. 1976, and the ceramic experts and scholars of the Palace Museum investigated the kiln twice. By materials of published and fact-finding, the thesis gives a brief introduction on glaze varieties, decoration features and firing history of Cicun kiln. Based on the analysis of relationship among Cicun kiln, local kilns and kilns near this area, the article confirmed that the porcelain produced by Cicun kiln has similar decorative method with kilns in northern part of China due to the influence of famous kilns in Hebei, Henan, etc. On account of absorbed the vanguard technology, the Cicun kiln made the porcelain full of unique flavor. The article also indicated the consistency of porcelain variety in high degree between Cicun kiln and kilns in southwest of Shandong.

宁夏灵武磁窑堡、回民巷古瓷窑遗址考察纪要

吕成龙

2005 年 11 月 23 日，笔者与故宫博物院古陶瓷研究中心的徐巍、郭玉昆先生和保卫处的葛爱萍女士利用到宁夏回族自治区银川市出公差的机会，在宁夏固原博物馆延世忠馆长、石磊女士的陪同下，考察了灵武市（1996 年撤县设市）的磁窑堡和回民巷古瓷窑遗址。

初冬的银川已有几分寒意，清早一起床，我们就将带来的棉衣全部武装到身上，撩开窗帘向外望去，只见曙光普照，天气晴朗。心想，天公作美，给了我们一个跑窑址的机会。匆匆吃过早饭，我们就乘车向窑址奔去。出了银川市区，沿银川至青岛高速路行驶 41 公里后，车子驶下高速路。透过车窗玻璃向外望去，瞅见路边一块牌子上写着“古窑子”三个字，心想可能到了。但延世忠馆长说：“还不到，还要跑一段土路。”沿着崎岖不平的土路跑了大约 8 公里，驶过一座桥，车子突然停下。延馆长说：“下车吧，磁窑堡古窑址到了！”我走下车，放眼望去，顿时被眼前的景象惊呆了，只见干涸的河床里和附近的山坡上到处都散落着瓷片和窑具，场面蔚为壮观。大家立即分散开，各自捡拾着自己中意的标本。一个多小时后，我们又考察了位于磁窑堡窑址以北约 4 公里的回民巷古窑址。

一 磁窑堡古瓷窑遗址

（一）地理环境

经查阅地图得知，灵武市位于宁夏中部偏北，黄河从县的西界流过，磁窑堡窑址在县城正东方向 35 公里处，南距磁窑堡镇（煤矿区）约 4 公里。从现场看，磁窑堡古窑址居于沙漠之中，大河子沟河自南向北经窑址西侧蜿蜒而过。河之东岸有一明代烽火台，为窑址区的最高点。窑址东侧有一干沟，属于季节河。窑址即位于干沟河和大河子沟河之间，南北长约 800 米，东西宽约 400 米。在干沟河的断崖上可以看到窑业堆积层厚达 2 ～ 4 米。回京后，经查阅有关资料得知，1983 ～ 1986 年中国社会科学院内蒙古工作队曾会同宁夏回族自治区博物馆对该窑址进行过调查和发掘[1]，采集和发掘出土了大量瓷器和窑具标本，基本弄清了该窑的烧造历史和烧造品种。经研究认为，磁窑堡窑创烧于西夏时期，元代仍在烧造。特别是该窑址所出土的大量西夏瓷器标本，对于研究宁夏、内蒙古、甘肃、青海等地出土的西夏瓷器提供了珍贵的实物资料。

（二）瓷器的品种

从考古工作者以往在窑址采集、发掘和我们这次在窑址采集的瓷片标本看，磁窑堡窑所烧造瓷器的品种比较丰富。按用途可分为生活用器、文房用器、娱乐用器、雕塑艺术品以及建筑用器等。若按釉色划分，则可分为白釉、黑釉、茶叶末釉、青釉、酱釉、姜黄釉等。供人们日常生活所使用的器皿有盘、碗、杯、盆、罐、钵、釜、瓮、盒、缸、壶、瓶、灯、铃、钩等，文房用器有砚台、砚滴等，娱乐用器有瓷埙、棋子等，雕塑艺术品有人物、动物等，建筑用有板瓦、筒瓦、瓦当、滴水等。窑址还散落不少“工”字形支烧用具，但窑址散落最多的是盘、碗残片。

（三）瓷器的装饰技法

磁窑堡窑瓷器所采用的装饰技法主要有划、剔划、点彩、雕塑等。白瓷系磁窑堡窑的大宗产品，从窑址散落的标本看，约占总数的一半以上，这可能与西夏王国崇尚白色有关。据文献记载，西夏的主体民族党项族发于白水之上，其国名即称“大白上国”或“白上大夏国”。但由于当地所出产瓷土含杂质较多，致使瓷器胎体不够洁白，多呈灰色、灰白色或米黄色。为此，瓷窑堡窑白瓷在施透明釉以前，均需先施一层洁白的瓷土（俗称“化妆土”），以遮盖坯体。因此，严格说来，磁窑堡窑白瓷与同时期北方定窑烧造的直接在胎体上施透明釉的白瓷不同，只能算作“化妆土白瓷”。其白瓷除了光素无纹饰者以外，也有采用划、剔划化妆土技法装饰者，即利用洁白的化妆土与颜色略深的胎体相互衬托进行装饰。划花系指用锥子划出图案纹饰，例如划出弦纹、卷草、婴戏、水波游鱼等。窑址出土一种白釉划花水波游鱼纹折沿盆，盆内壁划水波游鱼三尾，有的还在近口沿处划出卷草纹装饰带，鱼鳞是用戳印的排列有序的圆圈或半圆圈表示。整体装饰美观大方。剔划花是以剔花与划花技法相结合进行装饰，即器物成型后先施化妆土，然后用刀具剔掉纹饰以外的化妆土，再用锥子划出花卉的筋脉等细部，施透明釉入窑经高温烧成后，形成白地衬托深色花纹或深色地衬托白色图案的效果。磁窑堡窑白瓷的釉色不尽相同，有的洁白，有的则白中泛黄。

除了白釉瓷器以外，比较多见的是黑釉、茶叶末釉瓷器，这两种瓷器的釉料配方可能相同，之所以烧成后会形成不同的颜色，或许与烧成温度有关，即温度较高时，烧成黑釉，温度较低时烧成茶叶末釉。黑釉、茶叶末釉瓷器除了光素无纹饰者以外，也有不少采用划、剔划釉技法进行装饰者，其原理与划、剔划化妆土相似，只不过是利用釉色与胎色形成鲜明对比，装饰效果较强。黑色也是党项族所崇尚的颜色，据清吴广成《西夏书事》记载："德明三子，长元昊……元昊性雄毅，多大略，好衣长袖绯衣，冠黑冠，佩弓、矢。每出乘马，令从卫步足张青盖，以二旗前导，百余蕃骑自随。"[2]西夏太子元昊平时戴黑冠、出行令侍从张青盖，表明党项族崇尚黑色。

磁窑堡窑瓷器还有使用点彩技法装饰者，主要用于白釉或青釉碗、盘、盆等器物上，其做法是在器物施釉晾干后，以毛笔蘸黑褐色釉彩在器内涂点由斑点组成的图案纹饰，如以五个斑点组成梅花花朵或以九个斑点组成菱形纹，给人以简洁明快的视觉感受。

（四）磁窑堡窑瓷器的装饰题材

磁窑堡窑瓷器上的装饰题材主要是花卉纹和弦纹，也有人物纹、动物纹等。多以划、剔划花技法予以体现。西夏时期磁窑堡窑所烧造的剔划花瓷器上常使用开光装饰手法，开光的形状有菱形、海棠花形、四方形、括号形、连弧形等。开光内装饰牡丹、莲花等，开光以外的隙地上多以锥子划出表现海水纹的细密线条，颇具时代特色。其构图简洁大方，给人以质朴、粗犷、豪放的艺术享受。

这次我们在磁窑堡窑址还采集到一片刻划西夏文的匣钵残片，其上留有一个基本完整的西夏文字，其含义还有待于西夏文专家破解。带西夏文的西夏瓷器并不很多见，在李进兴先生撰《西夏瓷器》一书中收录两件造型相同施釉均不到底的双系瓶：一施黑釉，出土地点不明，瓶体刻划四个西夏文字，西夏文专家释其意为"富贵俱足"；一施茶叶末釉，系宁夏海原县西夏遗址出土，瓶体刻划两个西夏文字，译成汉语是"天都"二字[3]。上海博物馆收藏一件黑釉小口瓶，施釉不到底，腹部刻划五个西夏文字[4]。1984年中国社会科学院考古研究所内蒙古工作队在发掘磁窑堡窑址时曾发现两块署有墨书西夏文的褐釉碗残片[5]。甘肃省武威市古城乡塔儿庄曾出土一件施半截褐色釉的剔花翁，其白色胎上署有四行墨书西夏文，西夏文专家释其意为"斜毁"、"发酵有（裂）伤"、"下速斜"、"小"。这些西夏文瓷器的发现，对于西夏瓷器的断代具有重要意义。

（五）元代的磁窑堡窑

曾参加过磁窑堡窑遗址发掘的马文宽先生曾根据遗址地层的叠压关系分析认为，元代磁窑堡窑的烧造规模仍很大，但与西夏时期相比，其产品种类和造型品种均有所减少，质量也有所下降，胎质变得更加粗厚[6]。在装饰方面，元代磁窑堡窑瓷器中以划花、剔划花装饰者虽仍占有一定比例，但风格有了很大变化，装饰题材由西夏时的精致变为粗放简单，西夏时期那种开光剔划花装饰且开光以外的隙地上划出细密海水纹的装饰手法已基本不见，而变为简单的带状剔划花装饰。

二 回民巷古瓷窑遗址

回民巷古瓷窑遗址位于磁窑堡古瓷窑遗址以北偏东方向约四公里处。经查阅有关文献得知，1987年中国社会科学院考古研究所内蒙古工作队曾对该窑址进行过调查[7]。1997年宁夏回族自治区文物考古研究所、灵武市文物管理所为配合陕宁天然气输气管道工程施工，曾对该窑址进行过抢救性清理发掘[8]。基本搞清了该窑的烧造历史、烧造品种、装饰特色、工艺渊源等。该窑址位于磁窑堡镇回民巷村西侧的山梁上，在南北长约400米、东西宽约200米的范围内，瓷器残片和窑具标本俯拾皆是。

从窑址发掘和调查所获得的标本看，该窑所烧造的瓷器品种主要有黑釉、白釉、青釉、姜黄釉，另有少量褐釉、茶叶末釉、酱釉等。器物造型以碗、盘最为多见，另有罐、瓶、执壶、釜、缸、钵、炉、挂钩等。瓷器胎体坚硬，多呈灰白或黄白色，含有较多杂质。因此，其白釉瓷亦属“化妆土白瓷”，即在施透明釉之前，先在胎体上挂一层洁白的瓷土，以遮盖不太洁净的胎体。白瓷碗、盘均器内施满釉，外壁施釉不到底，俗称“半截釉”。内底有一周因使用细沙粒垫烧而留下的“砂圈”。碗、盘圈足有的较干净，有的则粘有较多沙粒。回民巷窑白釉瓷上有使用涂点褐斑装饰者，从这次采集到的白釉瓷盆残片看，其外壁涂抹酱色釉，内壁白釉地上有酱色釉斑组成的菱形纹饰。

其青釉瓷则不施化妆土，系在胎体上直接挂釉，釉层较薄，釉的透明度较好，呈淡淡的青色，透过釉层可以清楚地看到胎体上的疵点。青釉碗、盘外壁施釉均不到底，器内施满釉，但内底均有一周因刮釉叠烧而留下的“涩圈”，这与白釉碗、盘使用沙粒垫烧的做法明显不同。有的青釉盘、碗呈六瓣花式，与花式相对应的内壁有6条竖直凸棱，将盘、碗的内壁分成6等份。有的青釉盘、碗则仅在内壁有6条凸棱，口边却没有花口。上述磁窑堡窑烧造白釉划花水波游鱼纹盆，回民巷窑则烧造青釉划花水波游鱼纹盆。

从采集的标本看，回民巷窑所烧黑釉瓷的产量也很大，其胎色灰白，釉色多漆黑发亮，见有碗、盘、盏、钵、罐、执壶、器盖等。

姜黄釉瓷见有双系小罐、盒盖、碗等残片。姜黄釉印花瓷系该窑的特色产品，这次发现不少碗片，其印纹清晰，釉层较薄，釉面光亮，碗内施满釉，内底有涩圈，外壁施釉不到底。所印图案为缠枝花卉。

这次采集到的茶叶末釉瓷数量不多，仅有4片，可看出其造型有碗、罐等。釉色有深有浅，个别釉色纯正者，其外观效果不亚于清代景德镇御窑厂所烧造的同类产品。碗外壁施半截釉，内施满釉，内底有一周因刮釉叠烧而留下的涩圈。

在窑址还采集到一些“工”字形支具、顶碗等窑具。“工”字形支具有大有小，均系用手捏制而成，胎质坚硬，胎色灰白。顶碗呈上口小、下口大的喇叭形，系拉坯成型，胎色黄白。

三 调查的收获和认识

磁窑堡窑和回民巷窑相距仅4公里，两窑所烧瓷器既有联系又有区别。联系方面，两窑所烧瓷器质量、造型和花色品种等相类似，产品的成型、施釉工艺特征等相类似，所出产的划花水波鱼纹盆的装饰工艺亦相类似。区别方面，回民巷窑所烧造的黑、褐、青釉盘、碗当中，那种六瓣花式且内壁均匀分布6条凸棱的装饰技法是磁窑堡窑瓷器中所不见的。姜黄釉、青釉印花碗标本在回民巷窑址发现较多，但在磁窑堡窑址却极少发现。在磁窑堡窑址发现大量黑釉、茶叶末釉、白釉剔划花瓷器，在回民巷窑址极少发现。总的说来，回民巷窑瓷器具有装饰简单、粗率的特点，磁窑堡窑瓷器则具有装饰较复杂、细腻的特点。由于这两处窑址均经过局部科学发掘，考古工作者根据地层叠压关系和出土瓷器标本的类型学排比，将磁窑堡窑址所出土遗物分为五期，其中一期、二期为西夏中晚期，三期、四期、五期为元、明、清时期[9]。回民巷窑出土遗物则被分为早、晚两期，而且认为回民巷窑的晚期相当于磁窑堡窑一期，而回民巷窑早期比磁窑堡窑一期略早[10]。

关于磁窑堡窑和回民巷窑瓷器的工艺渊源，马文宽先生认为除“直接受到山西诸窑的影响外，还直接或间接地受到陕西、河北诸窑的影响”。笔者认为其受到山西介休、浑源、大同、太原等瓷窑影响的可能性更大。因为从瓷器的胎釉特征和装饰风格来看，磁窑堡窑和回民巷窑产品更接近山西诸窑产品。况且在1127年金灭北宋后，西夏与金保持了80年的友好关系，西夏与金的边界设有榷场，当时山西在金人的控制下，山西诸窑的瓷器必定会通过榷场贸易大量流入西夏，而史书记载西夏使臣往返金廷络绎不绝，西夏向金廷乞取制瓷匠人也是顺理成章的。

西夏（1038 ～ 1227年）是11 ～ 13世纪以党项族为主体建立的政权。因其地处我国疆域的西北部，故史称西夏。在其存在的189年中，曾先后和北宋（960 ～ 1127年）、辽（916 ～ 1125年）、南宋（1127 ～ 1279年）、金（1115 ～ 1234年）鼎足而立。疆域东尽黄河，西界玉门，南接萧关，北控大漠，即今宁夏全部、甘肃大部、陕西北部、青海和内蒙古部分地区。虽然西夏王国曾拥有广袤的领土、完备的典章制度，并创造过辉煌灿烂的民族文化，但是，元朝修正史时，西夏史则付诸阙如，仅于列传中略加叙述。致使西夏史料因未被系统整理而逐渐遗失。在这种情况下，深入挖掘、整理、研究西夏文物是十分必要的。

在1982年由文物出版社出版的《中国陶瓷史》和1994年由上海古籍出版社出版的《中国陶瓷》等讲述中国陶瓷发展史的权威论著中，对西夏陶瓷均未论及。虽然从20世纪60年代开始，在对西夏遗址发掘过程中，不断有西夏陶瓷出土，但人们真正对西夏陶瓷有比较清楚的认识，还是从20世纪80年代前期考古工作者对宁夏灵武磁窑堡窑址进行调查与发掘以后开始的。而1987年和1997年考古工作者对灵武回民巷窑所分别进行的调查与发掘，则进一步揭开了西夏瓷器的神秘面纱。

从考古调查所了解的情况来看，西夏陶瓷窑址除了磁窑堡、回民巷以外，还有银川市缸瓷井、灵武市石沟驿、贺兰县插旗口等，但无论是生产规模还是产品种类、质量，均以磁窑堡窑和回民巷窑为最。

1949年以来，故宫博物院曾派人对全国20个省、自治区的300余处重要窑址进行过调查并采集回6万多片瓷器标本，但这次故宫博物院工作人员对宁夏灵武磁窑堡、回民巷瓷窑遗址进行调查，尚属首次。它既填补了故宫博物院在古陶瓷窑址调查方面的一项空白，也为我们从故宫博物院陶瓷藏品中辨认西夏陶瓷提供了可靠的实物标本。

（该文原发表于《故宫博物院原刊》2006年第4期。）

注释：

1 中国社会科学院考古研究所内蒙古工作队：《宁夏灵武县磁窑堡瓷窑址调查》，《考古》1986 年第 1 期；中国社会科学院内蒙古工作队：《宁夏灵武县磁窑堡瓷窑址发掘简报》，《考古》1987 年第 10 期；马文宽：《宁夏灵武窑》，紫禁城出版社，1988 年。

2（清）吴广成：《西夏书事》卷四二，辑入《续修四库全书》史部第 334 册。

3 李进兴：《西夏瓷器》，宁夏人民出版社，2003 年；李进兴：《西夏文双耳小瓶》，《中国文物报》2001 年 8 月 22 日。

4 国家文物局主编：《中国文物精华大辞典——陶瓷卷》图 528，上海辞书出版社、商务印书馆（香港）有限公司，1995 年。

5 中国社会科学院考古研究所内蒙古工作队：《宁夏灵武县磁窑堡瓷窑址发掘简报》，《考古》1987 年第 10 期。

6 马文宽：《宁夏灵武窑》，紫禁城出版社，1988 年。

7 中国社会科学院考古研究所内蒙古工作队：《宁夏灵武县回民巷瓷窑址调查》，《考古》1991 年第 3 期。

8 孙昌盛、杜玉冰、余军、杨蕤：《宁夏灵武市回民巷西夏窑址的发掘》，《考古》2002 年第 8 期。

9 中国社会科学院考古研究所编著：《宁夏灵武窑发掘报告》，中国大百科全书出版社，1995 年。

10 孙昌盛、杜玉冰、余军、杨蕤：《宁夏灵武市回民巷西夏窑址的发掘》，《考古》2002 年第 8 期；中国社会科学院考古研究所编著：《宁夏灵武窑发掘报告》，中国大百科全书出版社，1995 年。

Abstract of the Investigation on Ancient Kilns of Huiminxiang and Ciyaobao at Lingwu in Ningxia Hui Autonomous Region

Lü Chenglong

Based on the collected specimens of investigation in ancient Ciyaobao kiln and Huiminxiang kiln at Lingwu in Ningxia Hui Autonomous Region and existing research achievement, the thesis discussed the porcelain varieties, culture meaning and artifact origin of the two kilns. The variety of porcelain in Ciyaobao kiln was comparatively rich, including staple goods, writing articles, sportful tools, figures and architectural terra cottas, etc. By glaze, the varieties included white glaze, black glaze, tea-dust glaze, celadon, dark reddish glaze, brown glaze, ginger glaze, etc. The decorative methods included incised design, carved design, color design and figure, etc. The pattern contented floral, string, human figure and animal, etc. The white glaze wares were the mainstream, probably due to the advocate white color by the Western Xia. The main product of Huiminxiang kiln included black glaze, white glaze, celadon, ginger glaze, brown glaze, tea-dust glaze, etc. The type included bowl, plate, jar, vase, pot with handle, vat, burner, etc.As the most important two kilns of Western Xia, the investigation and excavation of Ciyaobao kiln and Huiminxiang kiln provided us with valuable materials for porcelain dating and kiln judgment on remains of Western Xia in Ningxia, Inner Mongolia, Qianhai, and also precious historical material for the further study on history of Western Xia. It was a kind of tradition that launches the fact-finding for ancient kilns by the Palace Museum, and also a new path for study on ancient Chinese porcelain. The investigation fills the void of research on ancient kilns and enriched the specimens of ancient porcelain in the collection of the Palace Museum.

浅论西夏的磁州窑类型器

黄卫文 蔡毅

宋、辽、金时期，北方地区的瓷业生产十分繁荣，而地处西北先后与宋、辽、金并立的西夏王朝，制瓷业亦很发达。以前由于文献记载的缺失和资料匮乏，人们对西夏制瓷面貌的认识曾比较模糊。20世纪80年代以后，在一系列窑址调查与考古发掘新资料的支持下，古陶瓷研究者对西夏瓷的认识逐渐清晰。现有资料表明，西夏王朝的瓷业生产受到北方地区耀州窑、定窑、磁州窑制瓷的深刻影响，其产品在具有自身民族和地域特色同时，在制作工艺、烧制品种和器物装饰上更有着宋、金时磁州窑类型瓷器的许多特点，显然西夏瓷业发展与磁州窑应有密切的联系。本文依据现有窑址调查、传世及考古发现的材料，试对以宁夏灵武磁窑堡窑和甘肃武威塔儿湾窑为代表的西夏瓷中磁州窑类型产品的生产工艺、产品特征以及它们在北方磁州窑类型器中所独有的地域和民族特色等问题做一定的分析探讨。

一 宋、金时期的磁州窑类型器

在前代发展基础上，宋、金时期的北方瓷业生产更为繁荣。迄今文物工作者在今河北、河南、山西、山东、陕西、宁夏、内蒙古、北京等地区都发现了众多宋、金时期制瓷规模很大的古代窑场，这些窑场中“基础条件好的，烧造技术精良的，质量上乘的，具有特殊风格的有着丰富的原料和燃料资源，以及具有良好的商品交易环境的地区，逐渐被人们广泛接受，并且受到人们的称赞，被临近地区的瓷窑相继竞相模仿、学习”[1]。而磁州窑就是这样一处以自己特殊的产品风格与浓厚民间艺术气息装饰特色而吸引南、北各地窑场纷纷仿效的北方著名的民间瓷窑。

磁州窑窑址在今河北省邯郸市磁县的观台镇、彭城镇一带和峰峰矿区，两地宋代均属磁州，故名。磁州窑制瓷约始自五代末北宋初期，并一直延续至今，历史长达一千多年。宋、金时期是磁州窑制瓷的鼎盛期，此时的磁州窑不仅生产的瓷器品种丰富，器形实用多样，而且在胎体施加白色化妆土的基础上，利用绘画、划花、刻花、剔花、印塑、彩釉等多种多样的装饰技法，来表现极具民间风俗、风情的装饰内容。磁州窑以其质朴、洒脱、奔放的民间艺术装饰风格，影响到了北方地区许多瓷窑的制瓷生产，各地瓷窑纷纷模仿它的产品风格，生产了众多与磁州窑制品具有相同或类似工艺特征与装饰风格，可称“磁州窑类型”的瓷器产品。如河南鹤壁集窑、修武当阳峪窑、禹县的扒村窑、登封曲河窑，山西介休窑、霍县窑，山东淄博窑，江西吉安吉州窑，福建泉州窑，四川广元窑等都烧造过磁州窑类型的产品。作为先后与宋、辽、金并立，雄踞西北的西夏王朝，其制瓷业发展也受到了磁州窑的深刻影响。迄今，文物考古工作者已发掘了西夏时期的三处古瓷窑址，即宁夏灵武磁窑堡窑[2]、回民巷窑[3]和甘肃武威塔儿湾窑[4]，这三处窑址的调查与发掘，为我们初步揭示了西夏王朝制瓷历史发展的真实面貌。其中磁窑堡窑和塔儿湾窑堪称是代表西夏王朝制瓷水平的两处重要窑址，它们的产品在工艺特征、釉色品种、器形种类、装饰技法、纹饰图案等方面都与宋、金北方窑场生产的磁州窑类型瓷器有着相同或近似的风格，但由于窑场所处地域、工艺技术水平、民族生活习俗的不同，它们生产的磁州窑类型产品与北方其他窑场生产的磁州窑类型器物相比更具自身的地域和民族特征。

二 西夏制瓷业发展的历史背景

西夏王朝（1038 年～ 1227 年）是以党项羌人为主体，雄踞西北地区长达 190 年的一个政权。西夏自称“大夏”，因在赵宋王朝的西部，史称“西夏”。西夏都城为兴庆府（今宁夏银川市），其统治范围最大时包括今宁夏全境，甘肃的大部以及青海、内蒙古、陕西的部分地区，其疆域方圆数千里，东尽黄河，西至玉门，南界萧关（今宁夏同心南），北控大漠，幅员辽阔。兴起于西北游牧地区的党项羌人原本以牧业和狩猎为生，经济并不发达，经过对宋王朝的多次战争，相继侵占了物产丰饶，农业比较发达的原属宋的灵州（今宁夏灵武市）、凉州（今甘肃武威）和瓜州（今甘肃安西）等地。党项羌人开始学习汉人的农业技术，发展农业生产。由于农、牧业的发展，社会生产力迅速提高，西夏的手工业生产和商业贸易也随之发展起来。冶炼、陶瓷、纺织、造纸、印刷、酿造、采盐制盐、金银木器制作等手工业生产都具有一定的规模和水平。总体上看，西夏的经济是以半农半牧的生产方式为主，经济发展程度和规模与中原王朝相比仍显落后。历史上，西夏与宋、辽、金之间曾多次处于战争或对峙状态，其相对落后的经济显然不能支持长期的战争，因此西夏除了通过对外战争掠夺资源外，更依赖于与其他地区特别是北方中原地区的贸易往来补充财力和促进自身的经济发展。这一点突出表现在对宋朝“岁赐”与“和市”之上。史载：“既绝岁赐，复禁和市，羌中穷困，一绢之直，至十余千。既通和市，复许入贡，使者一至，赐予不赀，贩易而归，获利无算；传闻羌中得此厚利，父子兄弟始有生理。”[5]可见宋断绝与西夏的贸易往来，西夏境内便物价飞涨，穷困异常，反之才“始有生理”。这说明西夏的经济发展确实十方依赖于以宋王朝为代表的北方中原地区。

西夏王朝疆域内本身极度缺乏铜、铁等金属矿产，靠掠夺或贸易得来的金属资源十分有限，而有限的资源要用来制作武器或上层社会使用的金属器，人们日常的生活用具则要依赖木器或陶瓷器等。可见西夏社会生活对瓷器有着巨大的需求，这种需求有相当一部分是通过战争掠夺或贸易输入以满足，因此在和中原王朝的贸易中，瓷器占据了很大比重。但显而易见，瓷器作为一种生活必需品完全依赖外来输入几乎是不可能的，何况这种输入还经常受到断绝的威胁，因此在西夏王朝地域内也应该有烧制瓷器的窑场。而这些窑场处于何地？生产情况和产品特征怎样？以前由于文献记载的缺失和资料匮乏，研究者对西夏制瓷发展面貌的认识比较模糊，原西夏疆域内所发现的陶瓷制品，一般被定为宋、辽、金瓷器，或被视为元代产品，以至 1980 年前后编写的《中国陶瓷史》中，并无西夏瓷的有关描述。

三 西夏瓷窑址调查与考古发现

从 1949 年后发现的材料来看，西夏地域内瓷窑生产的瓷器即“西夏瓷”也曾零星有所发现。如 1956 年内蒙古伊金霍洛旗敏盖乡曾发现两件黑釉剔刻花瓶，其特征与宋代中原地区瓷器有一定的差异，被认为“可能与西夏有关”[6]。1964 年宁夏考古工作队在石咀（嘴）山市西夏“省嵬城”遗址发掘出土了玉壶春瓶、碗、罐、人头像等瓷器，其中人头像做秃发状，与党项羌人的习俗相同[7]。此后，在西夏时期的窖藏、墓葬和遗址中又陆续发现了一些资料，如西夏王陵区[8]、灵武崇兴乡窖藏[9]，甘肃武威西郊窖藏[10]和墓葬[11]，青海海东窖藏[12]，内蒙古伊金霍洛旗窖藏[13]、准格尔旗窖藏[14]，以及上海博物馆藏刻西夏文黑釉小口瓶[15]等。此外，在故宫博物院藏品中也收藏有数件西夏瓷，如宁夏博物馆拨交的灵武窑白釉碗，灵武窑窑址采集的青釉碗，传世的灵武窑黑釉剔花瓶、白地黑花猴鹿纹瓶、白地黑花折枝牡丹诗句纹瓶，以及与武威塔儿湾窑出土器相似的褐釉四系瓶等。上述考古发现或传世的瓷器，因为它们的制品特征既具有中原地区所产瓷器的特点，但又有所不同而逐渐被研究者认为可能就是陶瓷史中消失了的“西夏瓷”，并由此开展了寻找西夏制瓷窑场遗址的工作。

1983 年，中国社会科学院考古研究所在内蒙古额济纳旗的居延汉代烽燧遗址考察时，得到不少西夏至元代的遗物。考古人员对出土的一些瓷器进行分析后认为，这些瓷器应非远途运输之物。他们联系到灵武崇兴乡窖藏出土的瓷器，推测灵武境内可能有瓷窑遗址存在[16]。此后，社科院考古所的马文宽先生，依据《嘉靖宁夏新志》中“瓷窑山，灵州东北 60 里，为陶冶之所”[17]的线索，在古灵州即今宁夏自治区灵武县县城以东 35 公里、距磁窑堡镇西北 4 公里处终于找到了瓷窑遗址[18]，并将其命名为灵武窑。1984 年至 1986 年，社科院考古所对该窑址进行了 3 次系统的发掘，共清理西夏窑炉 3 座、西夏瓷器作坊 8 座、元代瓷器作坊 1 座、清代窑炉 1 座，发掘面积约 700 平方米。出土瓷器、瓷具、窑具共 3000 余件，同时发掘出大量墨书西夏文瓷片、墨书汉文西夏年款的瓷片和西夏钱币[19]。灵武磁窑堡窑址的发掘成果表明，灵武窑制瓷历经了西夏、元、明三个朝代，其中“西夏时期的产品种类繁多，以用途分类有生活器皿、文房器具、娱乐用品、雕塑艺术品、建筑材料、兵器等；以釉色分则有白釉、青釉、黑釉、褐釉、茶叶末釉和数量较少的紫釉，还有的一器施两种釉色，如外施黑釉、内施青釉的碗等；以装饰技法分有素釉、刻釉、剔刻釉、刻化妆土、剔刻化妆土、印花、点彩和雕塑等”[20]。灵武窑的调查发掘正式确认了“西夏瓷”的存在，并初步揭示了其产品特征和时代分期，使得文物工作者对西夏瓷的研究有了突破性的进展。

20 世纪 80 年代磁窑堡窑发掘之后，文物工作者又在灵武磁窑堡以北约 4 公里的回民巷、贺兰山东麓的缸瓮井、插旗口，甘肃武威塔儿湾及内蒙古伊金霍洛旗、准格尔旗等地发现了西夏时期的瓷窑遗址，并发掘了回民巷窑址[21]和塔儿湾窑址[22]。2006 年故宫博物院的专家在赴西北地区进行古代窑址调查工作时也曾调查了磁窑堡、回民巷、塔儿湾三处窑址，并采集到了重要的窑址标本。

从考古发掘和故宫博物院窑址调查取得的材料来看，西夏王朝的制瓷业是在当时北方地区定窑、磁州窑、耀州窑制瓷的影响下，结合自身民族和地域的特点发展起来的，其中灵武回民巷窑的产品主要受耀州窑的影响，以生产青黄釉刻划花制品为主，而灵武磁窑堡窑与武威塔儿湾窑生产的产品在制作工艺、釉色品种和装饰技法上都有着宋、金时磁州窑类型瓷器的产品特征，受北方磁州窑的影响十分明显。特别值得一提的是，故宫博物院的专家在调查西北地区窑址时发现，武威塔儿湾窑的产品不仅制作工艺比较精良，器形丰富，装饰多样，既有鲜明的磁州窑类型器特征，又有自身的地域、民族风格，流传的地域也很广阔，在甘肃、青海各级文物考古单位收藏的西夏遗址出土瓷器中常见有塔儿湾窑的产品。因此，可以说武威塔儿湾窑是继灵武磁窑堡窑之后，值得我们今后重点研究的又一处西夏瓷窑址。

甘肃省武威地区古称“凉州”，是古代丝绸之路上汉地通往西域的交通要冲，自汉唐以来一直是西北地区的重要政治、军事中心。塔儿湾窑位于“武威市城南 35 公里的古城乡上河村一组。这里地处杂木河上游，两岸依山。遗址分布在南岸的山坡和一片台地上，其中部分辟为农田，现已耕种。遗址东西长约 500 米，南北宽约 260 米，以西为草木茂盛的山区牧场，以东杂木河两岸是开阔的平原农田”[23]。塔儿湾因窑址附近河湾处建有一座白塔而得名，因地处偏远和交通不便，目前居民仅有十多户人家，使得当地的历史文化遗存保存较好。西夏时期，这里是党项羌人放牧、从事手工业生产和居住的地方。目前窑址附近仍有近代的制瓷窑场，据《武威县志》此地产“……石炭……煤……磁器；杂税……磁窑、煤炭税银二十两八钱”[24]。早在 1982 年甘肃省考古研究所就在塔儿湾发现了新石器时代的遗址，并在考古清理遗址工作时发现了大批的西夏瓷器[25]。1992 年至 1993 年上半年，甘肃省考古所对塔儿湾西夏文化遗址进行了考古发掘，发现了西夏时期的房屋村落遗迹，并出土了大量西夏时期烧制的各种瓷器、瓷片、窑具和烧窑留下的灰层堆积物，但因当时在考古工作中未能找到窑炉，发掘者仅将该遗址视为我国迄今发现的保存最完整的西夏村落遗址。然而从发现众多釉色繁杂、装饰多样的瓷器、瓷片和大量匣钵、支垫窑具，以及烧窑留下的灰层堆积物等现象判断，塔儿湾无疑应是一处西夏时期制瓷规模很大的窑址。

塔儿湾窑的产品风格与灵武磁窑堡窑类似，风格粗犷，一般器形较大，器胎较厚，并施有化妆土，施釉外不到底，底足无釉。釉色品种以白釉、黑釉为主，兼有绿釉、黄釉、褐釉。器形有盘、碗、高足碗、钵、扁壶、罐、双耳瓶、四系瓶、六系瓶、花式瓶、玉壶春瓶、缸、瓮、瓷人、瓷马等，装饰技法以刻花、剔刻花、白地黑花、点彩等为主，特别是白地黑花器发现较多，制作精良，画风质朴洒脱，为西北地区古代窑址中所罕见。纹饰常见缠枝牡丹、折枝牡丹、菊花、莲花、梅花点、牡丹飞禽纹等。

四 磁窑堡窑和塔儿湾窑西夏瓷的产品特征

灵武磁窑堡窑和武威塔儿湾窑的制瓷原料采用的都是各自当地产的青矸土，即“高岭石质泥岩”和“高岭石质泥夹矸”，这种瓷土是与煤层伴生的优质制瓷原料之一。器胎可分粗、细两类，粗者为杂质较多的砂、缸胎，细的胎土淘练比较精细，胎质较为细腻，但两者都给人胎质偏软的感觉。其胎色多呈浅黄或灰白色，为掩盖较差的胎色，胎体上一般都施有白色化妆土。

两窑西夏瓷的器物种类按用途可分为生活器皿、文房用具、娱乐用品、瓷塑及建筑材料等，常见器形有碗、盘、壶、瓶、罐、盆、灯、帐钩、纺轮、砚、铃、牛头埙、棋子、板瓦、滴水、人像、骆驼、马、鸡、鸭等。其中有些器形，如扁壶、多系（二系、四系或六系）瓶、帐钩、纺轮、牛头埙等是适应党项羌人游牧生活的特殊器形。以扁壶为例，其壶式可分两种，较大者为三圈足扁壶，壶小口、短颈、扁圆腹，腹部两侧中央均有圆形圈足，底亦为圈足，可正或两面平放，腹侧上下分别置两耳或四耳。该壶有三个圈足的特殊器形为西夏瓷所独有，三面均可置放，支撑稳当，腹侧有耳供穿带，将壶系带于马背，骑马出行时装水、酒携带十分方便。另一种扁壶略小，器形与大型扁壶相似，但无圈足，腹侧置双耳，只为随身携带使用。此外，两个窑址都发现很多宽系的二系、四系或六系瓶标本，器形也很有特点，如塔儿湾窑四系瓶、六系瓶，盘口，束颈，溜肩，鼓腹，圈足或平底，肩腹处饰四耳或六耳，耳部出棱，与北方其他窑场的带系瓶相比，系部明显较宽，系带更为结实牢靠，应为适应党项羌人游牧生活的需要而制成。而瓷帐钩、纺轮等则是西夏缺乏金属矿产，瓷器在社会生活中应用得更加广泛的表现。其他如两个窑址出土物中都发现了秃发人物的瓷像，更是与党项羌人的生活习俗有关，史载西夏开国皇帝李元昊在其建国前就发布过“秃发令”，规定“如三日不从令，许众杀之”[26]。

两个窑场烧制的品种以釉色分，主要以白釉、黑（褐）釉为主，也有少量青釉、茶叶末釉瓷器，多数外施釉不到底，有些器物里外釉色不同，底足一般无釉。其中白瓷质量普遍较高，精品亦多。器物装饰除一色釉器外，常用白地绘黑花、剔刻花、印花、点彩和雕塑等装饰技法，其中绝大部分壶、瓶、罐、钵等都采用剔刻花结合开光的装饰技法。这种剔刻花技法从工艺上可细分为刻釉、剔刻釉、刻化妆土、剔刻化妆土四种，具体来说，刻釉是在施釉的坯体上以刻刀在釉上刻划出花纹，花纹处露出胎色；剔刻釉则是在釉面上刻出纹饰后，再剔掉纹饰之外的釉层露出胎体，剔掉胎体使纹饰突出的做法颇有浅浮雕的效果，装饰效果极强；刻化妆土和剔刻化妆土与刻、剔刻釉工艺过程相似，只是在未施釉而只施化妆土的胎体上剔、刻纹饰，再罩上透明釉烧成。它们的装饰效果都是利用胎色与釉色或白色化妆土的色差来突出纹饰，对比鲜明。此外，剔刻花技法还结合有多种形式的开光使用，常见菱形、长方形、圆形或扇面形的开光，其中菱形开光采用得最多。

两窑产品的纹饰题材内容丰富，有植物纹、动物纹、婴戏纹及反映民间生活习俗的狩猎图。植物花纹中以折枝、缠枝或串枝牡丹纹最多，亦有折枝、串枝莲花纹、梅花纹、菊花纹等。动物纹有飞禽、鱼、蜜蜂和鹿纹等。故宫博物院亦藏有西夏白地黑花猴鹿纹瓶，高 42.5 厘米，口径 7.8 厘米，底径 12.7 厘米。小口微外卷，短束颈，溜肩，肩以下渐敛至底，平底无釉。外壁上下施褐釉，腹部饰白釉褐花纹饰，一面绘猴鹿纹，另一面饰飞禽纹，飞禽的画法与塔儿湾窑出土白地黑花牡丹飞禽纹瓶的纹饰画风颇为相似，很可能是塔儿湾窑的产品。此外，两个窑址出土器物标本中部分器物有墨书或划刻的文字、符号等，一般写在足内、肩部或腹下部，文字有汉文、西夏文、藏文等多种，是研究西夏文字的珍贵材料。

五 西夏瓷与北方磁州窑类型器的关系

宁夏灵武磁窑堡窑和甘肃武威塔儿湾窑的调查和发掘，为我们揭示了西夏瓷业发展的真实历史面貌。这两个代表西夏制瓷水平的窑场，烧制的产品在工艺特征、釉色品种、器形、装饰技法、纹饰图案等方面都与北方宋、金时期磁州窑类型器有着相同或相似的风格，但由于窑场所处地域、工艺技术水平、民族生活习俗的不同，产品特征与北方其他窑场的磁州窑类型器相比既有时代的共性又有自身地域和民族特点。

磁州窑的制瓷原料为当地多与煤层伴生的“大青土”，制胎时淘练得不够精细，颗粒粗，杂质高，胎色呈灰白或灰褐色。为适应粗瓷细作的需要，磁州窑器多在胎面上施加了白色化妆土，以遮盖其胎体表面的缺陷，从而提高瓷器的外观质量和釉的白度及光亮度。磁窑堡窑和塔儿湾窑的西夏瓷产品与磁州窑一样，采用的也是当地与煤层伴生的瓷土，胎质较粗，胎色多为浅黄色或棕黄色，为掩盖较差的胎色也使用了北方磁州窑类型器施白色化妆土的方法。在装烧方法上，宋、金磁州窑装烧方法有多种，民间使用的大路瓷多采用支钉、支垫垫烧，精细器用匣钵装烧，碗、盘有的用支圈或支垫一匣多器仰烧；还有用顶碗覆烧法，即用支顶碗（盘）放在筒式匣钵最底部起支撑作用，其他器物一层层向下叠着覆烧，此法烧成的碗、盘可克服瓷器芒口的缺陷，但内底往往有一圈粘砂或无釉现象。西夏瓷的装烧方法亦与磁州窑类似，盘、碗等有支钉、支圈正烧和匣钵正烧或顶碗覆烧法，为了增加装窑量，有的在罐上再扣上一件器物覆烧，因此罐类器物肩部常见一圈涩胎。

两个窑场西夏瓷的釉色品种虽无磁州窑丰富，但也以北方磁州窑类型最常见的白釉、黑釉、白地黑花等品种为主。而北方宋、金时磁州窑类型器中的许多器形，如花式瓶、玉壶春瓶、黑釉双耳罐等在两个窑场出土品中也能找到，只是器形略有差异。在装烧技法上，两个窑场都大量运用了剔刻花的工艺，塔儿湾窑还烧制了许多白地黑花的器物，而白地黑花和剔刻花正是北方磁州窑类型器最经典的装饰技法。与北方其他窑场的同类器相比，西夏剔刻花瓷露胎的面积往往较多，纹饰布局显得比较疏朗，露出的浅黄或棕黄色胎色与北方其他瓷窑的产品多浅白或灰白的胎色区别明显。

磁州窑的纹饰题材极为丰富多彩，内容多反映民间的风俗、风情。题材有花卉、飞禽、人物山水，其中花卉题材中以牡丹花为最多。西夏瓷中折枝牡丹纹样使用得亦多，其画法往往左右对称，花朵较大，左右两侧由花叶衬托，图案构思与磁州窑基本相同。

总的来说，宁夏灵武磁窑堡窑和甘肃武威塔儿湾窑的西夏瓷在诸多方面都带有北方磁州窑类型器的产品特征，这说明它们制瓷业的发展确实受到了宋、金时期北方生产磁州窑类型器相关窑场的影响，甚至可以说其制瓷工匠很可能就是来自这些窑场。以灵武磁窑堡窑考古发掘为例，发掘者把磁窑堡窑出土的瓷器分为五期。一期时代为西夏中期偏晚，即崇宗晚期及仁宗前期，二期时代为西夏晚期，三期为元代，四期、五期更晚[27]。而一期地层即是该窑场的始烧期又是鼎盛期，品种丰富，延续时间长，文化堆积层厚，且产品特征具有鲜明的北方磁州窑类型器的特点。可见，刚开始建窑烧瓷就能以成熟的技术烧制诸多高质量的瓷器品种，在没有任何前期技术积累的情况下，应该是外来技术支持的结果。因此从该窑始烧年代（约相当于北方的金代初期）及制瓷技术水平分析，其制瓷伊始，就得到了北方烧制磁州窑类型器瓷窑工匠们的技术帮助，磁窑堡窑的西夏瓷才得以烧制成功。

有关西夏制瓷的创烧发展是否是外来工匠作用的结果，史籍中并无明确的记载，如从当时的历史情形来推测，无非有三种情况：

一为北方地区的制瓷工匠为谋生或躲避战乱而前往西夏地区，尤其是北宋末期，金兵多次南侵，北方地区许多窑场在战争中损毁，如河南扒村窑碑记中就提到战后众多窑场只“百存二、三”。

二是通过战争劫掠工匠，西夏在金天会二年（1124年）曾短暂攻占了晋西北黄河地区一带，其撤退时很可能就掠走了晋北擅烧黑釉剔花器窑场的工匠。这种通过战争劫掠经济发达地区财富和手工业工匠的行为，在我国古代游牧民族与中原王朝的战争历史中可谓屡见不鲜。

三是向中原王朝索取工匠，如司马光在其所著《涑水记闻》曾记道，宋仁宗嘉祐七年（1062年）西夏毅宗谅祚曾遣使向宋朝“乞国子监印书、释氏经一藏并译经僧及幞头、工人、伶官”[28]等，宋朝只答应给予国子监印书及经书和幞头，派遣译僧、工人、伶官等要求则遭到了宋朝的拒绝，但西夏手工业制造对中原王朝匠人的需求仍可见一斑。

其后，在西夏配合金朝灭掉北宋后，西夏与金曾和平相处达80余年，金朝派遣制瓷工匠等手工业工人前去西夏也是很有可能的。

六 结语

综上所述，现有窑址调查与考古资料表明，以宁夏灵武磁窑堡窑和甘肃武威塔儿湾窑为代表的西夏制瓷业，在其发展的初期就已出现了大量与宋、金时期北方磁州窑类型器有着相同或相似制作风格的产品。这证明西夏制瓷是在北方其他生产磁州窑类型器相关窑场的影响下发展起来的，西夏瓷显然受到了宋、金时期磁州窑的直接或间接的影响，西夏制瓷发展应与磁州窑有着密切的联系。与北方其他地区窑场生产的同类器相比，由于这两个窑场所处地域不同，特别是它们所产瓷器的使用对象有着自己的民族风俗和生活习惯，因此其磁州窑类型产品又具有自身的地域和民族特色。笔者认为依据考古学的器物类型学概念，经上述研究分析，我们似可把本文中涉及到的磁窑堡窑和塔儿湾窑生产的西夏瓷品种称为“磁州窑西夏类型”器。

注释：

1 蔡毅：《宋金北方白瓷的比较学研究》，《中国古代白瓷国际学术研讨会论文集》，上海博物馆编，2005 年。

2 中国社会科学院考古研究所内蒙古工作队：《宁夏灵武县磁窑堡瓷窑址发掘简报》，《考古》1987 年第 10 期。

3 孙昌盛、杜玉冰、余军、杨蕤：《宁夏灵武市回民巷西夏窑址的发掘》，《考古》2002 年第 8 期。

4 黎大祥：《武威塔儿湾西夏遗址》，《武威文史资料》第六辑，2000 年 12 月。

5 （清）吴广成：《西夏书事》卷七，上海古籍出版社，2005 年。

6 内蒙古文物工作队：《内蒙古文物资料选辑》页 173，内蒙古人民出版社，1964 年。

7 宁夏自治区展览馆：《宁夏石咀山市西夏城址的试掘》，《考古》1981 年第 1 期。

8 宁夏回族自治区博物馆：《西夏八号陵发掘简报》，《文物》1978 年第 8 期。

9 钟侃：《宁夏灵武县出土的西夏瓷器》，《文物》1986 年第 1 期。

10 钟长发：《武威出土一批西夏瓷器》，《文物》1981 年第 1 期。

11 宁笃学等：《甘肃武威西郊林场西夏墓清理》，《考古与文物》1980 年第 3 期；宁笃学：《武威西郊发现西夏墓》，《考古与文物》1984 年第 4 期。

12 许新国：《青海互助土族自治县发现宋代窖藏》，《文物资料丛刊》1983 年第 8 期。

13 高毅、王志平：《内蒙古伊金霍洛旗发现西夏窖藏文物》，《考古》1987 年第 12 期。

14 伊克昭盟文物工作站：《准格尔旗发现西夏窖藏》，《文物》1987 年第 8 期。

15 上海博物馆选编：《上海博物馆藏瓷选集》图六一，文物出版社，1979 年。

16 马文宽：《宁夏灵武窑》，紫禁城出版社，1988 年。

17 胡汝砺撰，管律重修：《嘉靖宁夏新志》，宁夏人民出版社，1982 年。

18 中国社会科学院考古研究所内蒙古工作队：《宁夏灵武县磁窑堡瓷窑址调查》，《考古》1986 年第 1 期。

19 中国社会科学院考古研究所内蒙古工作队：《宁夏灵武县磁窑堡瓷窑址发掘简报》，《考古》1987 年第 10 期。

20 马文宽：《宁夏灵武窑》，紫禁城出版社，1988 年。

21 孙昌盛、杜玉冰、余军、杨蕤：《宁夏灵武市回民巷西夏窑址的发掘》，《考古》2002 年第 8 期。

22 黎大祥：《武威塔儿湾西夏遗址》，《武威文史资料》第六辑，2000 年 12 月。

23 黎大祥：《武威塔儿湾西夏遗址》，《武威文史资料》第六辑，2000 年 12 月。

24（清）张玿美修，曾钧、魏奎光纂：《武威县志》第一卷《物产》，清乾隆十四年刻本。

25 甘肃省文物考古研究所：《武威塔儿湾新石器时代遗址及五坝山墓葬发掘简报》，《考古与文物》2004 年第 3 期。

26 李焘：《续资治通鉴长编》，中华书局，1985 年。

27 中国社会科学院考古研究所内蒙古工作队：《宁夏灵武县磁窑堡瓷窑址发掘简报》，《考古》1987 年第 10 期。

28（宋）司马光：《涑水记闻》卷九，解梁书院本。

Abstract of a Brief Discussion on Wares in Cizhou Sytle of Western Xia

Huang Weiwen　Cai Yi

The porcelain production of Northern China has reached its peak in Song, Liao and Jin dynasty, and the Western Xia was also developed on porcelain making. Supported by the results of kiln investigations and new materials from archaeological excavations, the understandings of Western Xia porcelain among the Chinese academic community of ancient ceramics studies became more clearly since 1980s. Based on the materials of investigation and excavation and taking Ciyaobao kiln of Lingwu in Ningxia Hui Autonomous Region and Ta'erwan kiln of Wuwei in Gansu Province for examples, the thesis tried to discussed the problems including the productive technology, porcelain feature of Cizhou type wares in Western Xia, and the unique location and national feature were also included. Many characters of production technologies, kinds of pottery firing, and porcelain decorating in Ciyaobao kiln of Lingwu in Ningxia Hui Autonomous Region and Ta'erwan kiln of Wuwei in Gansu Province which were the representative kilns of Western Xia porcelain are the same as or similar to those in the type of Cizhou Kiln of Song, Jin dynasty. Meanwhile, Western Xia porcelain also has its own regional features and national characteristics. It is considered that the adventure of Western Xia porcelain has been influenced by the production of Cizhou Kiln directly or indirectly. According to the above analysis and typology of archaeology, the author put the conclusion that the wares of Western Xia which produced in Ciyaobao kiln of Lingwu in Ningxia Hui Autonomous Region and Ta'erwan kiln of Wuwei in Gansu Province, could named for Western Xia type in Cizhou kiln.

窑址调查纪要

窑址	调查时间	调查人
北京		
龙泉务窑	2006.3	冯小琦　王健华　吕成龙　徐　巍
山东		
淄博窑	1976.12	冯先铭　叶喆民
	2000.8	冯小琦　吕成龙
	2006.10	冯小琦　董健丽　赵　山　李有来
曲阜窑	2006.10	冯小琦　董健丽　赵　山　李友来
临沂窑	2006.10	冯小琦　董健丽　赵　山　李友来
枣庄窑	2006.10	冯小琦　董健丽　赵　山　李友来
宁阳窑	2006.10	冯小琦　董健丽　赵　山　李友来
陕西		
耀州窑	1954.4	陈万里　冯先铭
	1957.5	陈万里　李辉柄
	1975.6	冯先铭　李辉柄
	1977.5	李辉柄　李知宴
	1986.4	冯先铭　冯小琦　王莉英　吕成龙
	2006.10	冯小琦　蔡　毅　赵　山　王桂林
玉华宫遗址	1977.5	李辉柄等
旬邑窑	1962.4	冯先铭　叶喆民
	1977.5	李辉柄　李知宴
	2006.10	冯小琦　蔡　毅　赵　山　王桂林
澄城窑	2006.10	冯小琦　蔡　毅　赵　山　王桂林
	2006.12	冯小琦　蔡　毅
宁夏		
灵武窑	2005.11	吕成龙　徐　巍　郭玉昆　葛爱萍
	2006.10	冯小琦　蔡　毅　赵　山　王桂林
辽宁		
辽阳窑	2006.10	冯小琦　董健丽　赵　山　李友来

后记

《故宫博物院藏中国古代窑址标本》一套书经过近20年的酝酿，今天终于要逐卷面世了。本书是由故宫博物院几代陶瓷研究者——陈万里、冯先铭、李辉柄、叶喆民、王莉英、叶佩兰、李知宴、何俊义、欧志培、刘兰华、李毅华、邵长波、杨静荣、冯小琦、蔡毅、刘伟、纪伟、董健丽、赵聪月、郑宏、高晓然、韩倩等深入考古第一线采集的众多标本汇集而成。这些标本的收集历经了半个多世纪，经过三次大的整理。第一次是在1988年，由冯先铭先生负责，参加者有刘兰华、冯小琦、纪伟，主要整理存放在故宫文华殿与研究室的标本；第二次是在2004年，由冯小琦负责，主要参加者有杨静荣、蔡毅、刘伟，是在第一次的基础上，把数十年散放在承乾宫、永寿宫等数处的标本集中整理。整理工作从搬运开始，逐个开箱、清洗，并分省按窑口进行编目；第三次从2008年至今，由冯小琦负责，董建丽、韩倩参加。在前两次的基础上，对所有标本进行重新排柜位，核对数字，特别是对2005年以后调查的标本进行整理、拍照，对前两次整理的遗留问题进行解决。窑址标本文字介绍以冯先铭先生关于古窑址的论述为基础，由冯小琦进行整理与补充。附图说明由徐巍、董健丽、韩倩、黄卫文完成。此书得以出版，特别要感谢各级领导的大力支持与协调，感谢陶瓷组全体同人的合作，感谢资料信息中心的全力支持与配合。感谢各地博物馆、考古部门以及各地文保单位对故宫窑址调查工作的大力支持。

编辑出版委员会

摄影

马小旋　赵山

图片资料

故宫博物院资料信息中心

责任编辑

万　钧

装帧设计

北京颂雅风文化传媒有限公司

郑子杰　陈晓晓